P9-CFJ-933

3 2109 00098 4121

John Willard Brister
Library
Memphis State University
Memphis, Tennessee

WITHDRAWAL

A
GLOSSARY
OF
INDEXING
TERMS

A
GLOSSARY
OF
INDEXING
TERMS

Brian Buchanan

CLIVE BINGLEY
LONDON

LINNET BOOKS
HAMDEN-CONN

FIRST PUBLISHED 1976 BY CLIVE BINGLEY LTD
16 PEMBRIDGE ROAD LONDON W11
SIMULTANEOUSLY PUBLISHED IN THE USA BY LINNET BOOKS
AN IMPRINT OF THE SHOE STRING PRESS INC
995 SHERMAN AVENUE HAMDEN CONNECTICUT 06514
SET IN 10 ON 12 POINT UNIVERS MEDIUM
PHOTOSET PRINTED AND BOUND IN GREAT BRITAIN BY
REDWOOD BURN LTD TROWBRIDGE AND ESHER
COPYRIGHT © BRIAN BUCHANAN 1976
ALL RIGHTS RESERVED
CLIVE BINGLEY ISBN: 0–85157–208–1
LINNET BOOKS ISBN: 0–208–01377–6

Library of Congress Cataloging in Publication Data

Buchanan, Brian.
    A glossary of indexing terms.

    Bibliography: p.
    1. Cataloging—Dictionaries. 2. Indexing—Dictionaries. I. Title.
Z1006.B86 1976   025.3'03   75–20312
ISBN 0–208–01377–6 (Linnet Books)

Reference
Z
1006
B 86
1976

'Definitions are a kind of scratching, and generally leave a sore place more sore than it was before.'
Samuel (Erewhon) Butler: *Note-books*

Introduction

A specialist vocabulary enables us to think clearly about the concepts which are peculiar to our subject, and to communicate easily with our colleagues working in the same field. Without precise labels ideas are likely to remain vague and ill-defined—naming them crystallises them; and until we name them, we can only express ideas by periphrasis, which is tedious, wasteful and mind-clogging. A name is also evocative: it acquires helpful associations which a flat descriptive phrase, however accurately it represents the concept, can never have. There are, however, two difficulties about specialist vocabularies: they have to be learned, and there has to be agreement about the meaning of terms and as to which synonym is to be preferred for a concept.

The special language of indexing is necessary for the reasons given above; but students find it difficult to learn, and there is considerable inconsistency in usage among authors and lecturers in the subject.

This glossary attempts to overcome both problems. It is an enlarged version of a word-list provided for students at Loughborough School of Librarianship, who have found it useful to have formal definitions with explanations and examples available. The definitions reflect the author's usage, but are in general accepted by all indexing lecturers at Loughborough so that there is uniformity in usage in the school and in the Department of Library and Information Studies of Loughborough University of Technology. It is hoped that the glossary will provide the basis for more general agreement on the terminology of indexing.

The terms chosen for inclusion are those thought to be necessary when discussing indexing at basic levels: people doing advanced work should be familiar with all the terms included. There are a number of deliberate ommissions, as well as (no doubt) some inadvertent ones; for example, no proper

7

names have been included, so that there is no information about particular classification schemes or other indexing tools—unless the tool provides a convenient example of a generally-applicable indexing system (as does *British technology index*) or the name has lost the force of a proper name (as has PRECIS); similarly, terms which merely represent particular examples of a general concept are avoided—there is an entry for Common facets, but not for Standard subdivisions or General auxiliaries. On the other hand, when the concept is peculiar to a particular tool but may have general application it is included; examples include SC's General subjects and CC's Canonical classes. The other important omission is of terms whose meaning seemed to be too obvious to warrant inclusion—for example, Author headings, Title catalogues—or whose meaning is too close to that of an allied term—for example, Compound subject/Compound class.

Synonyms have been preferred on the basis of consensus, but this has been tempered by the need to avoid homographs or near-homographs, which cause confusion; for example, Multi-word subject has been preferred to the more generally accepted Compound subject; Polytopical work has been preferred to Composite work.

Entries are arranged in word-by-word order. Abbreviations in the form of separate initials are filed at the beginning of the appropriate letter sequence (for example, there is a reference from BTI, at the beginning of the B sequence); but those in the form of acronyms are filed as words, so that SLIC is found between SIZE and SOUGHT HEADING. The two headings filed under numerals form the first two entries in the glossary.

There may be up to three parts in each entry; the first, labelled a) is a basic definition with examples where necessary; the second, b) amplifies a) with a· fuller explanation or more examples; the third, c) refers the user to related terms other than those already mentioned in a) and b).

See references are made from synonyms and near-synonyms to preferred terms, and also from terms involved in the definition of other terms where the repetition of information seemed to be unnecessary (eg Leap in division *see* Modulation).

The abbreviations for the names of classification schemes used in the glossary are as follows (a numeral following an abbreviation indicates the edition; eg LEC 1 = *London education classification* 1st ed). BC—*Bibliographic classification*; CC—

8

Colon classification; DC—*Decimal classification*; LC—*Library of Congress classification*; LEC—*London education classification*; SC—*Subject classification*; UDC—*Universal decimal classification*.

To ensure that the definitions given here were not too idiosyncratic, and that most common terms were included, the following standard works were consulted during the preparation of the glossary: AACR (British text) 1967; E J Coates *Subject catalogues* Library Association, 1960; A C Foskett *Subject approach to information* 2nd ed London, Clive Bingley; Hamden, Conn; Linnet Books, 1971; Alan Gilchrist *The thesaurus in retrieval* Aslib, 1971; John Horner *Cataloguing* Association of Assistant Librarians, 1970; International Conference on Cataloguing Principles *Report* 1963; F W Lancaster *Information retrieval systems* Wiley, 1968; F W Lancaster *Vocabulary control for information retrieval* Washington: Information Resources Press, 1972; Derek Langridge *Approach to classification for students of librarianship* London, Clive Bingley; Hamden, Conn, Linnet Books, 1973; J Mills *Modern outline of library classification* Chapman & Hall, 1960; S R Ranganathan *Prolegomena to library classification* 3rd ed Asia Publishing House, 1967; John R Sharp *Some fundamentals of information retrieval* Deutsch, 1965.

I must thank my three indexing colleagues at Loughborough—Ken Anderson, John Shinebourne and Fred Smith—for their interest in this glossary, and for their help in discussing definitions and reading drafts. I owe to a former colleague, David Hope, now librarian of the Welsh National Water Development Authority, the pleasant idea of aestivating dragons (see Difference), as well as a concern for precision in the use of our specialist language.

BB May 1975

7–4–2–1 CODING

a) A fixed-field indirect coding system for edge-notched cards. Each field consists of four holes labelled respectively 7, 4, 2 and 1; within each field any number from 0 to 9 may be encoded by opening those holes whose sum equals that number—the example shows three fields used to encode the number 576.

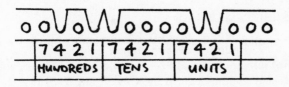

b) Economy in use of holes is achieved at the expense of false drops. These occur for two reasons: 1) because 0 is not positively encoded—absence of opened holes is taken to mean the digit 0—a search on 76 will also yield 576; and 2) because each hole may be used to encode more than one digit, a search on 576 will also yield 472, 174, 572 etc. Both causes are overcome by the use of 7–4–2–1–S–0 coding.

7–4–2–1–S–0 CODING

a) A coding system similar to 7–4–2–1, except that six holes are used, labelled appropriately, and that two holes are opened for each digit (except 0, for which hole 0 is opened). For the digits 7, 4, 2 and 1, which do not need two holes to make up their sum, hole S is opened in addition to the appropriate numbered hole. 0 is therefore positively encoded, and each digit from 1 to 9 has a unique pair of holes; false drops due to these causes are therefore avoided.

A

ABBREVIATED ENTRIES *see* ADDED ENTRIES; LIMITED CATALOGUING; UNIT ENTRIES

ABRIDGEMENT

a) A shortened version of a work, whose preparation has not involved re-writing or presentation in a different form.

c) Adaptation.

ACCESSIBILITY

a) A quality of physical forms of catalogue: the degree to which one user of a catalogue prevents others from using it.

ACCESSIBILITY MEASURE

a) The ratio $\dfrac{\text{number of entry terms}}{\text{number of index terms,}}$ which gives the average number of references for each entry term in an index vocabulary— one of the measures devised by Kochen and Tagliacozzo.

c) Approach term; Connectedness ratio.

ACCESSION NUMBER

a) A running number unique to each document, assigned by the library.

b) Used for administrative purposes, and, in some cases, as the basis for shelf order.

c) Book number; International Standard Book Number; Sequential order; Term entry systems.

ACCIDENT

a) One of the five predicables: an attribute which is not shared by all members of a species, and which therefore cannot be essential to its definition; eg, any cat may be ginger or tabby or black, without this attribute affecting its cat-ness.

b) If the literature of a subject field shows the need for inclusion of a class based on accident then it must be provided for in the classification scheme. This shows that concepts important in logical classification are not always relevant to classification for indexing.

c) Artificial classification; Difference; Property.

ADAPTATION

a) A different presentation of an original, involving re-writing or change of form; eg, a work re-written to make it suitable for a

12

different audience (children, immigrants), or a work in the form of a film-script or a play based on a novel.

   c) Abridgement.

ADDED ENTRIES

   a) Entries made under headings of secondary importance; eg, if main entry is under author's name, added entries may be made under title of document, translator's name, series title etc.

   b) Added entries may be abbreviated for economy, if unit entry is not used.

   c) Analytical entries.

ALL THROUGH *see* LETTER BY LETTER

ALLOCATION

   a) The relative amount of notation allowed to parts of a classification scheme.

   b) Poor allocation results in long class numbers in areas which develop rapidly, such as technology, or in areas whose importance has been underestimated, and short notation in the favoured areas. DC provides notorious examples; eg logic uses numbers from 160 to 169, while electrical engineering is allowed only 621.3.

   c) Base; Brevity.

ALPHABETICAL SUBJECT CATALOGUE

   a) One whose headings are the names of subjects in ordinary language.

   c) Alphabetico-classed catalogue; Alphabetico-direct catalogue; Systematic catalogue; Syndetic structure.

ALPHABETICAL SUBJECT INDEX

   a) The index to the classified file of a systematic catalogue, or to the schedules of a classification scheme.

   c) Chain procedure; PRECIS; Relative index; Specific index.

ALPHABETICO-CLASSED CATALOGUE

   a) A pre-coordinate alphabetical subject catalogue within whose headings generic and similar relationships are displayed; eg Science—Chemistry—Inorganic (as opposed to Inorganic chemistry).

b) This form of catalogue abandons the direct approach—the main justification for alphabetical subject catalogues—and yet does not achieve collocation as effectively as the systematic catalogue.

c) Alphabetico-direct catalogue; Syndetic structure.

ALPHABETICO-DIRECT CATALOGUE

a) A pre-coordinate alphabetical subject catalogue whose headings are in direct form; that is, they do not attempt to display generic relationships; for example, an alphabetico-direct heading would be Pistols, not Firearms—Pistols; Inorganic chemistry, not Science—Chemistry—Inorganic.

b) This form provides direct access (it is sometimes said to be a 'one-approach' catalogue) provided that the enquirer happens to use the indexer's preferred term in his approach; but generic searches are tedious because of alphabetical scatter. References are used to guide enquirers from synonyms to preferred terms, and from related headings; eg Philately *see* Stamp collecting; Mathematics *see also* Arithmetic. When interfiled with an author-title catalogue, the alphabetico-direct catalogue forms a dictionary catalogue.

c) Alphabetico-classed catalogue; British Technology Index; Direct access; Divided catalogue; Prepositional phrases; Syndetic structure; Systematic catalogue.

ALPHABETICO-SPECIFIC CATALOGUE

a) An unhelpful synonym for alphabetico-direct catalogue: the difference between the alphabetico-classed and the alphabetico-direct catalogues is not one of specificity—both use equally specific headings—but of directness.

ALPHABETISATION

a) The process of putting in alphabetical order.

b) The problems involved include choice of word-by-word or letter-by-letter filing; how to file abbreviations; what to do about modified vowels (eg does Göthe file before or after Goth?) etc.

ALTERNATIVE ENTRIES

a) Unit entries with no headings.

b) These allow the local library to assign its own headings, without the need to take supplied headings into account when filing.

ALTERNATIVE TITLE
a) A title presented as an alternative to the main title by the use of the word 'or' on the title-page; eg *Hermsprong; or, Man as he is not.*

b) Alternative titles differ from sub-titles in that they cannot be considered part of the accepted title; although their explanatory functions may be similar.

AMPLIFIED PHRASES *see* PREPOSITIONAL PHRASES

ANALETS
a) Descriptors in the form of names of concepts joined by relational operators, in Farradane's relational indexing system; eg Hunting /: Firearms /— Decoration.

c) PRECIS.

ANALYTICAL ENTRIES
a) Added entries for parts of documents; eg, for each play in a volume of *Plays of the year*; for additional material by a different hand; for discrete subject areas covered, perhaps unexpectedly, by the document.

b) Analytical entries must obviously lead the enquirer to the document which contains the part, using a form such as

Leslie, *Sir* Shane A memoir *in* Symons, A J A *The quest for Corvo* . . .

c) Depth indexing.

ANALYTICO-SYNTHETIC CLASSIFICATION SCHEMES *see* FACETED CLASSIFICATION SCHEMES

AND *see* LOGICAL PRODUCT

ANNOTATION *see* NOTES

ANONYMOUS AUTHORSHIP
a) Unknown or insufficiently-identified authorship.

c) Uncertain authorship; Unnamed groups; Pseudonyms.

15

ANTONYMS

a) Words of opposite meaning; eg Wet/Dry, Good/Evil.

b) Antonyms may be confounded in index vocabularies so as to increase recall.

c) Synonyms.

APERTURE CARDS

a) Cards which frame a copy of the document indexed by the card, so that retrieval of the card also retrieves a version of the document.

b) This is an application of edge-notched cards. The document held in the card may be in microform, or a photograph of a painting etc.

APPROACH TERM

a) The term used by the enquirer when beginning his search in an information retrieval system; eg, 'What have you got on wireless engineering?'

b) The approach term may have to be converted into a preferred synonym or preferred word form when the index vocabulary is controlled.

c) Accessibility measure; Entry term.

APPROACH VOCABULARY *see* ENTRY VOCABULARY

ARBITRARY SYMBOLS

a) Notational symbols which have no obvious filing value; eg =
; " " () etc; as in 362(420) "1837/1901" (024.7) (ie a work for children on English social welfare in victorian time; notation from UDC).

b) Such symbols cannot be used alone, and certainly make the notation more difficult to understand; but they extend the notational base, and, used as facet indicators, enable a library to choose a citation order appropriate to its needs while maintaining broader-narrower order.

c) Flexibility(1); Inversion.

ARITHMETICAL NOTATION

a) Notation which is not divisible; for example, in LEC1 the notation consists of a capital letter followed by two lower-case letters (eg Fab, Jib) and division by the addition of more letters is not allowed.

b) Such notation is not hospitable; for example, consider the following sequence from LEC1:

Tig   Slow learning
Tik   Retarded
Til   Illiterate
Tim   Maladjusted

Suppose we wished to insert the class Dyslexic into the sequence, as a sub-class of Illiterate; it should follow Til and precede Tim, but no notation is available which would enable us to place it there. It could be placed in the gap between Tig and Tik (at Tih, say), but this would misplace it. To be truly hospitable, notation must be fractional; for example, the notation Tild would place the new class correctly.

c) Fractional notation; Gap notation.

ARRAY (1)
a) A set of coordinate classes in a classification scheme.
c) Order in array.

ARRAY (2)
a) All the classes which comprise a facet or sub-facet.

ARROWGRAPHS
a) Diagrammatic representation of relationships between concepts, with arrows linking related concepts, as in diagram on p. 18.
c) Circular thesaurus.

ARTICULATED SUBJECT INDEXING
a) M F Lynch's multiple entry system, which maintains meaning in each entry by observation of the position of prepositions. The indexer states the subject in the form of a prepositional phrase; eg *Effect on children of death*; the entry words are extracted, and the remainder of the phrase added to each; those parts of the phrase which end with a preposition come before the entry word's place; those which begin with a preposition come after: *Children, Effect on, of death; Death, Effect on children of*
b) The entries are produced by computer after the indexer has

constructed the basic prepositional phrase.

c) PRECIS.

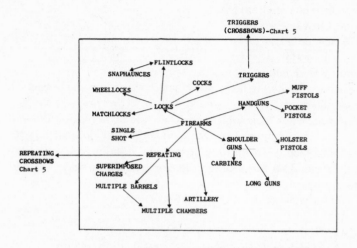

ARTIFICIAL CLASSIFICATION

a) Classification not based solely on the essential properties of things, and which therefore displays not only genus-species relationships but other kinds of relationship, such as Thing-part, Thing-operation.

b) Bibliographic classification is necessarily artificial, because it must display all the relationships which occur in documents or which may be expressed by enquirers; it is not enough to show the Firearm-pistol relationship—the classes Decoration of firearms and Firearm locks must also be capable of specification.

c) Accident; Natural classification.

ARTIFICIAL INDEXING LANGUAGES

a) Those which are controlled and structured as a result of work by the indexer.

c) Natural language indexing systems.

ASPECT CLASSIFICATION SCHEMES

a) General classification schemes based on conventional disciplines and specialisms; eg, a scheme with main classes such as Arts, Sciences, Technologies, Social sciences etc.

b) Most schemes are of this type—the major exception is the obsolete SC, which is based on concretes rather than disciplines. Aspect classification schemes provide expected groupings, reflecting division of labour, and so are helpful to enquirers; but concretes—entities—are scattered in various aspects (Children may be found in Law, Psychology, Medicine, Social welfare etc; Coal in Geology, Economics, Fuel technology etc); and it may be difficult to place a general work which is on all aspects of a thing.

c) Concretes; Fundamental class; General subjects; One-place classification schemes.

ASSOCIATION MAPS *see* ARROWGRAPHS

ASSOCIATIVE RETRIEVAL SYSTEMS

a) Mechanised indexing systems which rely upon counts of the co-occurrence of terms as the basis for grouping.

c) Chains; Clumps; Stars; Stings.

ATTRIBUTE

a) A quality essential to the definition of something.

c) Accident; Property.

ATTRIBUTED AUTHORSHIP *see* UNCERTAIN AUTHORSHIP

ATTRIBUTES

a) The qualities and actions on and of things, as opposed to the things themselves.

b) The CRG general classification scheme was intended to have only two facets; an Entities (things) facet and an Attributes facet. This was based on Barbara Kyle's work on the classification of the social sciences; but Brown's SC had a similar distinction—between concretes and general subjects—much earlier.

ATTRITION

a) The practice of cataloguing new accessions according to a

19

new policy, while maintaining a single catalogue, and re-cataloguing existing entries only when they conflict with a new entry.

c) No conflict; Superimposition.

AUGMENTED KEYWORD INDEXES *see* ENRICHED KEYWORD INDEXES

AUTHOR

a) The creator of a work; the person or corporate body respon-sible for the content and presentation of a work.

b) Responsibility for a work need not imply that any part has been written by the person concerned; for example, a work pro-duced under editorial direction may be said to be the responsibility of the editor, who may have contributed nothing to the actual text. Authorship is a less important concept for indexers today: the growth of new media in which authorship may be diffuse, or may not provide a sought heading, and the use of computers, lead to the idea of providing entry-points under any sought label, whether this is an author's name, a performer's name, a person responsible for the document rather than the work etc.

c) Compiler; Corporate author; Intellectual responsibility; Joint authorship; Primary author; Principal author; Secondary author; Subsidiary author.

AUTHOR UNIT *see* BIBLIOGRAPHIC UNIT

AUTHORITY FILE

a) A record of cataloguing decisions made in a particular library, kept to ensure consistency in practice.

B

BTI *see* BRITISH TECHNOLOGY INDEX

BASE

a) The number of symbols available for use in the notation of a classification scheme.

b) The longer the base, the shorter the notation for any class is likely to be. The length of base is principally determined by the number of different symbols available in the set—obviously a pure notation using the alphabet is likely to have a longer base than one using pure numerals. However, other factors may have an effect: if flexibility is provided by the reservation of more than one notation for the same class the base is shortened, as it is if a minimum length of class number is specified—for example, if a minimum of three letters is required then all two and one letter notations are wasted: FAB may be used, but not FA or F. A peculiarity of alphabetical notations is that unacceptable combinations of letters must be avoided (after all, one of the desired qualities of notation is that it should be easily said!) and this also reduces the base.

c) Allocation; Arbitrary symbols; Brevity; Mixed notation.

BASIC CLASS

a) A class which represents a discrete area of knowledge in which one could specialize.

c) Canonical class; Main class.

BATCH PROCESSING

a) Searching a computer store for a number of requests at once, the requests having been accumulated over some time.

b) Batch processing is more economical than direct access, especially where the volume of requests is small compared to the size of the data base.

BATTEN CARDS *see* OPTICAL COINCIDENCE CARDS

BERGHOFFER FILING

a) Filing under authors' names, but ignoring forenames and initials; so that within entries under a particular surname, filing is by document title.

b) This is supposed to make the use of the catalogue as a finding list easier, and it certainly makes filing easier; but it reduces the value of the catalogue as a bibliographic catalogue. It is for these reasons often used in union catalogues.

BIAS

a) The reflection of social attitudes, or of local needs, in the construction or use of indexing tools; eg, detail in DC's Area Tables for the USA; CC's emphasis on Eastern religions.

c) Critical indexing; Favoured category.

BIAS PHASE RELATIONSHIP

a) The relationship between the subject of a document and the persons for whom its special presentation is intended; shown in titles such as *Ballistics for police officers; Arithmetic for nurses; Logic for librarians.*

b) The citation order is Subject–For whom intended; but it is sometimes difficult to decide whether one has a bias phase or a quasi-generic relationship; for example, is a work entitled *Police mathematics* about mathematics in general, especially presented for police officers, or is it about a *branch* of mathematics?

An objection to the concept of bias phase relationships is that, unlike other phase relationships, the documents in which they occur give no information—or very little information—about the secondary phase; for example, if *Police mathematics* were an example of bias phase one would learn very little about police work from it. For this reason it might be better to consider the bias phase as a form of presentation rather than a true phase—as, indeed UDC does, with its form division (024)—books for special types of user.

c) Complex classes.

BIBLIOGRAPHIC CATALOGUE (1)

a) One which displays bibliographical relationships by collocation—eg by the use of uniform headings for authors—at the expense of its finding-list function.

b) For example: *Eros denied* is by Wayland Young; *Preservation* is by Wayland Kennett. These are two names for the same man. If we enter both under a uniform heading, eg Kennett, Wayland Young, *Viscount* the relationship between the works, as being by the same author, is displayed, and the enquirer who wants all works by Lord Kennett is satisfied; but the enquirer who knows that *Eros denied* is by Wayland Young and searches for it under that name finds only the irritating reference; Young, Wayland, *Viscount Kennett, see* Kennett, Wayland Young, *Viscount*

c) Berghoffer filing; Collocative catalogue; Uniform headings; Unit of collocation.

BIBLIOGRAPHIC CATALOGUE (2)

a) One which serves as a bibliography, because of the comprehensiveness and standing of the collection it represents.

BIBLIOGRAPHIC COUPLING

a) Grouping documents according to the number of other documents they cite in common in their bibliographies.

b) A computerised technique.

c) Citation indexing.

BIBLIOGRAPHIC FORM *see* FORMS OF PRESENTATION; PHYSICAL FORMS OF DOCUMENTS

BIBLIOGRAPHIC UNIT (1)

a) The document in hand to be indexed, as opposed to the work of which it is a manifestation.

c) Literary unit.

BIBLIOGRAPHIC UNIT (2) *see* UNIT OF COLLOCATION

BIBLIOGRAPHIC WARRANT *see* LITERARY WARRANT

BIBLIOGRAPHY

a) A list of works or documents (or both), usually with some relationship between them—eg, by the same author, on the same subject, published in the same place; or cited as sources or further reading by the author of another work.

b) This is the generic term; a catalogue is a kind of bibliography—one which lists documents related by inclusion in the same collection.

c) Bibliographic catalogue (2)

BINARY CODING

a) A fixed-field indirect coding system for edge-notched cards. The holes are labelled with powers of two (ie 2^0, 2^1, 2^2, 2^3 etc), and those holes whose sum equals the number to be encoded are clipped open; eg, 7 would be encoded by opening the holes 2^0 $(=1)$, 2^1 $(=2)$, and 2^2 $(=4)$.

b) Binary coding is very economical in use of holes—10 holes enable over 1,000 numbers to be encoded; but a high proportion of false drops is inevitable, as the same power of two may the component of many numbers. Again, for some numbers a large number of holes must be clipped open—and searched; eg 15 is encoded by opening holes 2^0, 2^1, 2^2, and 2^3; while 478 uses holes 2^1, 2^2, 2^3, 2^4, 2^6, 2^7 and 2^8.

BOOK FORM CATALOGUE

a) A catalogue in the form of a loose-leaf or a bound book, with several entries on each page.

b) Such catalogues are easy to scan, portable and psychologically acceptable; but difficult to update satisfactorily, until the computer and modern printing techniques made frequent new editions feasible.

c) Guardbook catalogue; Printed catalogue; Sheaf catalogue.

BOOK NUMBER

a) Notational symbols which are unique to an individual document, and give it a logical filing position in relation to other documents which are on the same subject.

b) Ranganathan says that the book number may consist of symbols for concepts from the following: language of document; form of document; year of publication; accession number; number of the volume; number of supplement; number of copy; a notation which represents 'criticism', for a criticism of a work; accession number of the critical work.

c) Call number; International standard book number; Shelf marks.

BOOLEAN ALGEBRA

a) The logical operations—logical difference, logical product and logical sum—which, when applied to a class, produce new classes. Formulated by George Boole in the mid-nineteenth century, these operations are the basis of symbolic logic; and of search strategy in information retrieval systems, as well as the logical basis of the digital computer.

c) Class inclusion; Venn diagrams.

BOUND TERMS *see* UNIT CONCEPTS

BREVITY

a) A desirable quality in notation—the briefer the notation for a class, the easier it is to use in filing, writing, remembering and locating.

b) Brevity depends on length of base and allocation of the notation; on whether the notation is hierarchical; on whether synthesis is used; and on the degree of specificity of the scheme.

BRITISH TECHNOLOGY INDEX

a) An index to periodicals which exemplifies the alphabetical subject cataloguing technique advocated by its editor, EJ Coates, in his *Subject catalogues*. The order of elements in what Coates calls compound headings corresponds to his significance formula Thing-part-material-action-property; eg Tyres: Cords; Polyester fibres: Safety.

Added entries are made to show the Whole-part relationship when it exists: Cords (Tyres); Polyester fibres: Safety. Inversion references provide access through the other elements: Safety: Polyester fibres; Cords: Tyres *see* Tyres: Cords; Polyester fibres: Safety. Polyester fibres; Cords: Tyres *see* Tyres: Cords; Polyester fibres.

In addition, references are made from synonyms and from superordinate and other related classes, eg Vehicles: Wheels related headings: Tyres.

BROAD CLASSIFICATION

a) To assign a document to a class of greater extension than the document's subject; eg, to place a work entitled *French flintlock hunting rifles* in the class Rifles.

b) Broad classification increases the recall performance of an indexing system at the expense of precision. This loss will not be important in small collections (although the possible future size of the collection must be considered when choosing the level of generality), and other considerations—such as ease of use for inexperienced readers—may be allowed to over-ride the need for precision. To facilitate shelving and locating documents, broad classification may be used for shelf order, leaving the catalogue to provide specificity.

c) Close classification; Generic entry; Segmentation.

BROADER-NARROWER ORDER

a) A helpful filing order in which no item on a narrower subject files before any on a broader; as in this sequence: Play therapy—Maladjustment—Play therapy for maladjustment—Children—Play therapy for children—Maladjusted children—Play therapy for maladjusted children—Adolescents etc.

b) Notice that broader-narrower order does not mean that all items which precede a given item are broader than it, nor that all which follow are narrower.

c) General-special order; Helpful order; Inversion; Narrower-broader order.

BROKEN ORDER

a) An interrupted sequence of documents is said to display broken order; as when all documents on appropriate subjects are removed from the main library to a subject department.

c) Parallel sequences.

BROWSING (1)

a) To look through a store of documents at random, with no conscious search strategy.

c) Serendipity.

BROWSING (2)

a) To choose from among a number of documents by examining each.

BYPASSING REFERENCES

a) Downward or upward references which, for economy in indexing and searching, do not modulate; eg: Mammals *see also* Man (not Mammals *see also* Primates; Primates *see also* Man)

c) Modulation.

C

CIP *see* CATALOGUING IN PUBLICATION; PRECATALOGUING

CALL NUMBER

a) A code unique to a document within a collection, which shows its shelf location—the code used to 'call' for the document.

b) Call numbers may include a sequence notation, classification notation and book number.

c) Shelf marks.

CANONICAL DIVISION

a) A conventional subdivision of a main class in CC, not derived by facet analysis, and with its own citation order; eg, the classes Arithmetic, Algebra, Geometry etc in the main class Mathematics; the classes Architecture, Sculpture, Graphics, Painting etc in Fine arts.

CANONICAL ORDER

a) An order in array sanctioned by usage outside the sphere of bibliographic classification; eg, the order of classes representing biological species could conform to that used by taxonomic biologists.

CARD CATALOGUE

a) Physical form of catalogue in which each entry is made on a separate card, the cards being interfiled.

b) Card catalogues have flexibility, and are easy to guide; but they are bulky, not portable, difficult to scan (only one entry is shown at a time), and one user may obscure many drawers.

c) Book form catalogue; Sheaf catalogue.

CASES

a) Particular manifestations of general author/title cataloguing problems; eg, if the general problem (or condition) is that of choice of name for an author with more than one, a case would be a nobleman as author, who has both a family name and a title (Wayland Young or Viscount Kennett?).

b) Since the work of Seymour Lubetzky the advantages of making rules for conditions rather than cases has been acknowledged.

CATALOGUE

a) A list of documents available in a particular collection, arranged in intelligible order.

c) Bibliographic catalogue; Bibliography; Index; Systematic catalogue.

CATALOGUE CODES
a) Published guides to the solution of problems in author/title cataloguing and descriptive cataloguing; eg the British Museum's *Rules . . .*, the Anglo-American Code of 1908, the Vatican Library's *Rules*, *Anglo-American cataloguing rules*, 1967, and *Non-book materials cataloguing rules* (LANCET).
c) Cases; Conditions.

CATALOGUING
a) The processes involved in constructing a catalogue: describing documents so as to identify and characterize them; providing entry points peculiar to the document—eg, author headings, title headings; and providing for subject and form approaches.

CATALOGUING IN PUBLICATION
a) A form of centralised cataloguing, in which cataloguing data is provided with the document.
b) Cataloguing in publication depends on pre-publication cataloguing, which requires cooperation from publishers, and carries with it the danger of changes in the document between cataloguing and publication. BNB currently (early 1975) refer to their proposed pre-publication cataloguing—intended to improve the currency of their services—as cataloguing in publication; this seems to be an unhelpful appropriation of a term whose other meaning is generally accepted.
c) Precataloguing.

CATALOGUING IN SOURCE *see* CATALOGUING IN PUBLICATION

CATCHWORD (1) *see* KEYWORD

CATCHWORD (2)
a) A displayed word used in guiding—eg, at the head of a page in a dictionary.
c) Feature heading.

CENTESIMAL NOTATION *see* GROUP NOTATION

CENTRALISED CATALOGUING
a) The production of cataloguing data by a central agency for

distribution to local libraries.

b) This prevents wasteful repetition of work, may lead to improved standards, and helps to produce uniformity in practice between libraries; but there may be a need for local variations in cataloguing practice, there may be delay in the supply of data, and the coverage of the centralised service may have gaps.

Centralised cataloguing data may be distributed in the form of a bibliography; as cards or sheaf slips; as cataloguing in publication; as computer input media; as information from a computer data base through on-line terminals; in the form of micromaterial.

c) Cooperative cataloguing; Precataloguing.

CHAIN

a) A sequence of classes in subordination;

c) Array; Chain procedure; Characteristics of division; Hierarchy; Steps of division; Subordinate class; Superordinate class.

CHAIN PROCEDURE

a) A technique for the construction of a relative alphabetical subject index developed by Ranganathan and popularised in this country by its use in BNB until 1970. The chain which ends in the class of the document to be indexed is analysed, and the term which represents each step of division which may be sought is used as an entry word in the index; where necessary, qualifiers are added to the term from those above it in the chain—the terms which represent its superordinate classes; and the appropriate notation is added. In addition, synonyms are indexed. For example, the chain:

```
Arms/Weapons           C
    Missile                2
        Guns/Firearms          4
            by lock                e
                Flintlocks             3
                    by use                 a
                        Hunting                8
```

would result in the following index entries:

1) Hunting flintlock firearms C24e3a8
2) Flintlock firearms C24e3
3) Firearms C24
4) Guns C24

5) Missile weapons C2

6) Weapons C

7) Arms C

b) Apart from indexing the classified file, this form of index dis plays relationships which are hidden by the classification scheme for example, not all works on hunting weapons would be found together—for example hunting swords might have the notation A4a8; hunting spears B2a8. In the index, entries such as Hunting Flintlocks C24e3a8; Hunting: Spears B2a8; Hunting Swords A4a8 would provide a means of correcting this separation.

Chain procedure is economical, avoiding unnecessary entries (that is, those entries which show a relationship already displayed by the classified file; eg, there is no entry in the index under Flintlocks: Hunting C24e3a8, because the entry at Flintlocks C24 would lead the enquirer to the subordinate class in the classified file, especially with good guiding); and it is usually a simple, near-mechanical process.

Chain procedure may be adapted to produce alphabetical subject catalogues, as Ranganathan suggested; the first entry in a) above could serve as a subject heading, while the remainder could provide generic references (eg Flintlocks *see also* Hunting: Flintlocks) or synonym references (eg Guns *see* Firearms).

c) Connective index entry; False links; Hidden links; Inversion references; Multiple entry indexing systems; PRECIS; Unsought links.

CHARACTERISATION

a) A function of descriptive cataloguing: in addition to identifying the document, the description may indicate what kind of document it is so that the enquirer can make a selection from the catalogue. Characterising information includes physical form, extent, level, imprint information etc.

c) Enrichment.

CHARACTERISTIC OF DIVISION

a) A property shared by members of a class which differentiates them from members of other classes, and which is used in the construction of classification schemes.

c) Facet; Focus; Logical division; Steps of division; Subfacet.

CHRONOLOGICAL ORDER

a) An order in array which depends on a time or developmental relationship; shown in the order Infants, Children, Adolescents, Adults; or in Romanesque, Gothic, Baroque; or Matchlock, Wheellock, Flintlock.

CIRCULAR THESAURUS

a) A visual display of genus-species relationships, in which the classes are shown in concentric circles about the genus, the distance from the centre indicating the number of steps the class is removed from the genus.

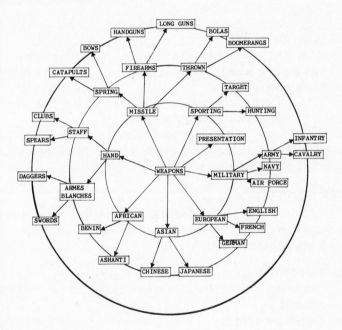

c) Arrowgraphs.

CITATION INDEXING

a) The grouping of works on the basis of their common citation of some other work. A citation index (such as *Science citation index*) is a list of cited works, each followed by a list of those works which have cited it.

b) This enables the enquirer to move forward from a known work to later related works (compare the function of citations at the end of a work: these enable the reader to go back to earlier works). The economy of this non-intellectual indexing technique is reduced by the need to supply other indexes to supplement the citation index; but computerisation makes it easy to provide alternative approaches.

In a standard work in our field the author cites *Pride and prejudice* in his list of references at the end of a chapter: this is an example of a minor drawback of citation indexing—it depends on the value of the citations!

c) Bibliographic coupling.

CITATION ORDER (1)

a) The order in which elements of notation are synthesised to express a superimposed or composite class, when using a faceted classification scheme.

b) Citation order determines collocation on shelves, and in single-entry systematic catalogues.

c) Consensus; Decreasing concreteness; Dependence; Distributed relatives; Facet formula; Filing order; Fundamental categories; Purpose; Standard citation order.

CITATION ORDER (2)

a) The order in which characteristics of division are applied to produce subclasses in an enumerative classification scheme.

b) & c) As Citation order (1)

CITATION ORDER (3)

a) The order in which elements in an alphabetical subject heading are placed.

c) Significance order.

CLASS (1)

a) A set whose members share a property not shared by members of other sets.

c) Boolean algebra; Characteristics of division; Connotation; Denotation; Extension; Logical division; Predicables.

CLASS (2)

a) The representation, in a classification scheme, of concepts which may be found in works, the use of which enables documents to be grouped in classes (in sense 1).

c) Canonical class; Collateral classes; Composite class; Coordinate classes; Main class; Partially comprehensive class; Simple class; Subordinate class; Superimposed class; Superordinate class.

CLASS INCLUSION

a) A relationship between classes such that one is wholly included in the other; eg, that between Adults and Middle-aged people, or that between Weapons and Firearms.

c) Common membership; Euler circles; Genus-species relationship; Logical sum.

CLASS INTERSECTION *see* COORDINATION; LOGICAL PRODUCT

CLASSED HEADING *see* GENERIC HEADING

CLASSIFICATION (1)

a) The process of recognising classes (1) and the relationships between them, involving one or more of the following activities: naming a concept, to distinguish it from other concepts; establishing the relationships between concepts; displaying those relationships; displaying those relationships by systematic order; showing what that order is by the use of notation.

b) These activities are cumulative: the later depend on the earlier. By this definition any indexing system which uses a controlled and structured vocabulary is based upon classification—classification is not synonymous with classification schemes, nor with systematic order.

c) Boolean algebra; Characteristics of division; Collocation; Logical division; Predicables.

CLASSIFICATION (2)

a) The process of assigning documents to a class (2).

c) Classification by attraction.

CLASSIFICATION BY ATTRACTION

a) To assign a document to an incorrect class in a classification scheme, because that class is the only apparently specific one; eg, using LEC2, to place a document on the teaching of television engineering in the class Los (= television as a teaching aid) instead of in the correct but non-specific class Nav (= Teaching electronic engineering).

CLASSIFICATION SCHEME

a) A ready-made list of classes whose relationships are displayed by juxtaposition, and which is used to produce a systematic order of documents or of records of documents; eg DC, UDC, LEC, BC, CC.

b) The elements of a classification scheme are schedules; notation; and index.

c) Classification; Enumerative classification scheme; Faceted classification scheme; General classification scheme; Special classification scheme.

CLASSIFIED CATALOGUE

a) A systematic catalogue whose headings consist of notation from a classification scheme.

c) Classified file; Feature heading; Relative index.

CLASSIFIED FILE

a) The subject component of a classified catalogue, in which entries for documents are arranged according to notation from a classification scheme.

CLIQUES

a) Karen Sparck Jones's name for groups of terms derived by associative indexing techniques in which each term is connected with each other term.

c) Clumps; Stars; Strings.

CLOSE CLASSIFICATION

a) To assign a document to a class (2) which is co-extensive with its subject.

b) Close classification increases the precision performance of an indexing system, but decreases recall.

To simplify shelving, documents might be given broad classification, leaving close classification to the classified file.

c) Specificity; Verbal extension.

CLOSED ACCESS

a) Used of a store of documents which users are not allowed to inspect, so that they must select from catalogues and bibliographies and ask assistants to fetch specific documents for them.

b) Closed access may be necessary for security reasons; it also saves space—there is no need to allow for circulation of readers in the store—and may allow a simple shelf order to be used, as readers are not going to select documents from the shelves. It is sometimes thought that closed access forces readers to make more rational choices of documents (it is for the same reason that some Scandinavian libraries bind books in uniform dull bindings), and it certainly ensures that they make some contact with the staff of the library. Conversely, the reader cannot make a choice by browsing among documents, which is a limitation on his freedom (but in any case browsing is not helpful for some forms of document—eg films).

c) Open access.

CLUMPS

a) Groups of associated terms based on their co-occurrence in texts, within which there are more connections between terms than between those terms and members of other clumps.

c) Associative retrieval systems; Cliques; Stars; Strings.

CLUSTERS *see* CLUMPS

CODE TERMS *see* DESCRIPTORS (2)

CODING

a) Opening holes on item entry cards to represent terms.

c) Direct coding; Fields (1); Indirect coding; Posting.

COEXTENSIVE

a) Specific; of equal extension. Used of subject descriptors in relation to the subjects of documents.

b) Close classification; Depth indexing; Generic entry; Specificity; Summarisation.

COLLABORATIVE AUTHORSHIP *see* JOINT AUTHORSHIP

COLLATERAL CLASSES

a) Classes which are of equal status in a hierarchy—that is, are the same number of steps of division down from a parent class—and are in the same subject area, but which do not share the same immediate superordinate class; eg, the class Radio is collateral with the class Newspapers in this hierarchy:

```
                    Mass media
     The Press    Broadcasting    The Cinema
     Newspapers    Radio    Television
```

c) Coordinate classes; Subordinate class; Superordinate class.

COLLATION

a) The description of a document as a physical object, in a catalogue entry.

c) Characterisation; Enrichment; Pagination; Plates.

COLLECTION

a) A document containing works, or parts of works, not originally intended for publication in the document.

c) Composite authorship; Editorial direction.

COLLOCATION

a) The bringing together or juxtaposition of related items so as to display their relationship, and to enable searches to be easily broadened, narrowed and extended.

c) Citation order; Classification; Collocative catalogues; Distributed relatives; Helpful order; Systematic order; Uniform headings.

COLLOCATIVE CATALOGUE

a) One which displays relationships between documents by juxtaposition of their entries.

c) Bibliographic catalogue (1); Syndetic catalogue; Systematic catalogue; Uniform headings; Unit of collocation.

COM see COMPUTER OUTPUT MICROFORM

COMBINATION INDEXING

a) A multiple entry indexing system, in which entry is made

under each of the sets of terms which may be derived by the omission of elements without changing their order; eg:

1) Cataloguing: Maps: University libraries. 2) Cataloguing: Maps 3) Cataloguing: University libraries 4) Cataloguing 5) Maps: University libraries 6) Maps 7) University libraries.

In addition, references from synonyms and from superordinate and other related terms must be made.

b) Only one entry is specific, but each element is juxtaposed with each other element (eg Cataloguing is juxtaposed with Maps in entries 1) and 2), but also with University libraries in 3)). In order to narrow a search, users must know the citation order of elements, so in an alphabetical subject catalogue using combination the order is usually alphabetical, as in the example in (a).

The number of entries generated by combination is given by 2^n-1, where n = the number of elements; with 3 elements, 7 entries are produced.

c) Cycling; Permutation indexing; Rotation; Shunting; SLIC.

COMBINATION ORDER *see* CITATION ORDER

COMMON FACETS

a) Facets which may be applied anywhere within a general classification scheme, and which are listed once only.

b) Common facets take concepts such as place, period, form of presentation etc; examples include UDC's General auxiliaries and BC's Systematic schedules.

c) Common subdivisions; Form classes; Generalia.

COMMON MEMBERSHIP

a) Classes which belong equally well in more than one other class form the common membership of those other classes; eg, the class Hunting spears is the common member of the classes Hunting weapons and Spears.

c) Composite class; Logical sum; Logical product; Mutually exclusive classes; Superimposed class.

COMMON SUBDIVISIONS

a) Subheadings which may be used with many headings in a subject headings list, and which are therefore listed separately, with instructions on how to add them as necessary.

  c) Common facets.

COMPARISON PHASE RELATIONSHIP

  a) A relationship in which one phase of a complex class is compared with another; eg Kayaks *compared with* Canadian canoes; *A comparison between* post-coordinate and pre-coordinate indexing systems.

  b) As this is a two-way relationship, or non-directional relationship (ie Kayaks *compared with* Canadian canoes means the same as Canadian canoes *compared with* kayaks), the choice of citation order is arbitrary; but it is usual to cite first the phase which files first in the classification scheme.

COMPLEMENTATION *see* LOGICAL DIFFERENCE

COMPLEX CLASS

  a) A composite class whose elements are in a phase relationship; that is, they remain distinct and separable, not fusing to form a permanent new class. Ranganathan's other term for this kind of class is 'loose assemblages'.

  b) For example: a document entitled *A comparison between steam and diesel locomotives* shows the temporary nature of the relationship—the class exists only in this document. Similarly, *The influence of the arts and crafts movement on the English house* is about two distinct subjects (it is not about the English arts and crafts house) loosely assembled in this document.

  c) Compound class.

COMPOSITE AUTHORSHIP

  a) The condition in which two or more authors have made distinguishable contributions to a work, the contributions having been especially written for it; eg, *A history of English architecture* by Peter Kidson, Peter Murray and Paul Thompson, for which Kidson wrote the section on the middle ages, Murray that covering the period from tudor to regency times, and Thompson the section on victorian and modern architecture.

  c) Collection; Editorial direction; Joint authorship; Mixed authorship.

COMPOSITE CLASSES

a) Classes composed of two or more elements in a relationship of interaction; eg Teaching French by the direct method in primary schools; Respiration of owls; A comparison between flintlock and snaphaunce guns.

b) Notice that the relationship does not define a *kind* of the elements involved—'respiration' is not a kind of 'owl', nor are 'owls' a kind of 'respiration'. The two kinds of composite class are complex and compound classes.

c) Simple class; Superimposed class.

COMPOSITE WORK *see* POLYTOPICAL WORK

COMPOUND CLASS

a) A composite class whose elements have their extension decreased by the relationship—they fuse to form a new subject from which the elements cannot be extricated; eg, the class Respiration of owls is of lesser extension than either of the classes Respiration or Owls, and the class represents not the subject 'respiration' and the subject 'owls', but 'the respiration of owls'.

b) In faceted classification schemes, compound classes are expressed by the synthesis of notation for foci from different facets.

c) Complex class; Simple class; Superimposed class.

COMPOUND SUBJECT (1)

a) Ranganathan's term for a basic subject plus one or more isolate ideas; eg Child psychology (basic subject Psychology, isolate idea Child).

c) Compound class.

COMPOUND SUBJECT (2) *see* MULTI-WORD SUBJECTS

COMPUTER OUTPUT MICROFORM

a) This form of output enables frequent production of new catalogues, at less cost than with conventional paper print-outs, and with much less waste material to be disposed of.

CONCEALED AUTHORSHIP

a) Anonymous or pseudonymous authorship.

CONCEPT INDEXING

a) The indexing of ideas rather than the terms used by an author to represent those ideas; controlled language indexing as opposed to natural language indexing.

c) Free indexing.

CONCEPT STRING

a) A subject descriptor in the form of terms linked by relational operators, used as the basis of entries in a PRECIS index; eg University libraries (1) Maps (p) Cataloguing (2).

c) Context dependency.

CONCEPTS

a) Ideas, as opposed to the terms which represent ideas.

c) Class; Concept indexing; Natural language indexing.

CONCRETENESS

a) The quality of being material, as opposed to abstract—eg 'map' is more concrete than 'cataloguing'.

c) Decreasing concreteness.

CONCRETES

a) Things, as opposed to properties of things, actions on things or aspects of things.

b) In J Kaiser's *Systematic indexing* the citation order Concretes-Processes is suggested; in J D Brown's SC concretes are collocated while aspects are scattered (eg works on Coal are collocated, and works on Mining are separated—some with general works on mining, some with coal, some with diamonds etc).

c) Aspect classification schemes; General subjects; One-place classification schemes.

CONDITIONAL EXCLUSION

a) A statement in the form 'A *but not* B *unless* C'; eg, 'I want information on flintlock firearms, excluding military firearms unless they are handguns'.

c) Logical difference; Optical coincidence cards.

CONDITIONS

a) General statements of author/title cataloguing problems, to which solutions can be suggested for the guidance of cataloguers faced with particular manifestations; eg a rule 'enter the works of an author who has used more than one name under that name by which he is better known' deals with a condition, while a rule 'enter the works of a woman who has written under both her married and her maiden name under the name by which she is better known' would be an example of a solution for a case, or manifestation of a condition.

b) Since Lubetzky's work, and the ICCP in 1961, the principle of providing for conditions rather than for cases has been accepted, although not in practice absolutely followed—as AACR shows.

CONFOUNDING

a) To control word-forms by the use of a preferred term.

c) Controlled index vocabularies; Paradigm; Truncation.

CONJUNCTION *see* LOGICAL PRODUCT

CONNECTEDNESS RATIO

a) The ratio $\dfrac{\text{number of terms connected to others by references}}{\text{total number of terms in index vocabulary}}$ suggested as a measure of the level of referencing in an index vocabulary by Kochen and Tagliacozzo.

c) Accessibility measure.

CONNECTIVE INDEX ENTRY

a) In a relative index to a classified file produced by chain procedure: an entry which abandons the principle of qualifying entry words by superordinate terms only, so as to reveal relationships obscured by defects in the classification scheme.

b) For example, two areas of the book-trade, publishing and bookselling, are badly separated in DC: Publishing in classes 655.4–655.5 and Bookselling in 658.809 001 552, separated by classes such as Accounting 657, Plant management 658.2 and Payroll administration 658.321. Conventional chain procedure entries would not correct this; instead, the theoretically incorrect entries; Book-trade: Bookselling 658.809 001 552, Book-trade: Publishing 655.4, could be added, to produce a helpful collocation of the names of related classes not otherwise possible.

c) Feature headings.

CONNOTATION

a) The set of properties essential to the definition of a class; eg the connotation of the class labelled Rifles is 'firearms with spirally grooved bores intended to spin the bullet'.

c) Denotation; Intension.

CONSENSUS

a) A guide to the choice of citation order: citation order should reflect the way in which the subject is taught or otherwise thought about by informed people; eg, it is usual to teach history in schools by place rather than by period—students do not usually study, say, the seventeenth century (in Europe, America, China, Russia, India etc), but rather Great Britain or wherever (in the seventeenth century, during the industrial revolution, between the world wars etc), so that this guide would suggest the citation order Place—Period.

c) Educational and scientific consensus.

CONSTRUCTED HEADING see STRUCTURED HEADING

CONTEXT DEPENDENCY

a) The principle on which order in the concept string for a PRECIS index is based, to ensure that each entry is meaningful: that each element should be contained by the element which precedes it in the string, and should contain that which follows it; eg Secondary schools—Curriculum—Geography—Teaching methods—Field work.

b) Context dependency order is produced by the use of relational operators which have an ordinal code.

CONTROLLED INDEX VOCABULARIES

a) Those which recognise and cope with synonyms, different word-forms and homographs, so that the enquirer is led to all available documents whichever synonym or word-form he has used, and is not led to irrelevant documents.

b) Control of synonyms and word-forms leads to increased recall performance; control of homographs leads to increased precision.

c) Classification scheme; Concept indexing; Confounding; Natural language indexing; Search thesaurus; Structured index vocabularies; Thesaurus.

CONVENTIONAL INTENSION *see* CONNOTATION

CONVENTIONAL TITLE
   a) A uniform title which states the document's subject or form in a standard format; eg
Burney, Fanny
   Correspondence
      The letters of Madame D'Arblay . . .
Mozart, W. A.
   Symphony no 41, C major, K 551 (Jupiter)
      Symphony in C major . . .

COOPERATIVE CATALOGUING
   a) The exchange of cataloguing data between libraries.
   c) Union catalogue.

COORDINATE CLASSES
   a) Classes of equal status in a hierarchy, which share the same immediate superordinate class; eg, main classes in conventional general classification schemes; CC's canonical classes; and classes produced by the application of the same characteristic of division. In the following hierarchy, the classes The Press, Broadcasting and Cinema are coordinate with each other, as are Radio and Television:

Mass media
The Press   Broadcasting   Cinema
Newspapers   Radio   Television

   b) Coordinate classes form an array.
   c) Collateral classes; Order in array; Subordinate classes; Superordinate classes.

COORDINATE INDEXING *see* POST-COORDINATE INDEXING SYSTEMS

COORDINATION
   a) The expression of the relationship 'A *and* B'—the logical product—in an indexing system.
   c) Composite classes; Post-coordinate indexing systems; Pre-coordinate indexing systems; Superimposed classes.

CORPORATE AUTHORSHIP

a) Authorship responsibility assumed by a group of people acting as a body rather than as individuals; eg learned societies; educational institutions; government bodies; commercial firms etc.

b) The concept of corporate authorship is still not readily accepted throughout the world; for example, countries of continental Europe prefer title entry for works for which English-speaking countries would use a corporate author heading.

c) Personal authorship.

CRITICAL INDEXING

a) The construction or use of indexing tools in such a way as to reflect social attitudes or national or cultural bias.

c) Favoured category.

CROSS-CLASSIFICATION

a) The provision of more than one apparently valid place for a subject in a classification scheme, with no indication as to which is to be preferred.

b) Cross-classification may occur through the provision of flexibility and its careless use. It may also happen through the fault of the scheme, if the maker of the scheme has applied more than one characteristic at a time—breaking a rule of logical division. Consider this sequence from LEC2:

Subdivide by educands beyond usual age of formal education
Swb Adult
Swd Parent
Swf Housewife
Swg Older person

It is obvious that the classes are not mutually exclusive—a parent may well also be a housewife and an older person—so that more than one characteristic has been applied to produce this array. As a result, what is one to do with a work on teenage parents at school? Is it to go at Svj (teenagers) or at Swd (parents)? It can hardly be given the notation Swd, because teenagers are not beyond the usual age of formal education, and yet the work needs to be collocated with other works on parents as students. Both places are equally unsatisfactory, and the indexer has to choose to ignore either the age element of the parenthood element; the specific notation SwdSvj is not possible, for the reason given above–teenagers cannot also be adults!

44

c) Logical division

CYCLING

a) A multiple specific entry indexing system in which each catalogue entry retains the same form, but different elements are used as the entry word; eg

DECORATION. Flintlock. Hunting. Rifles.

Decoration. FLINTLOCK. Hunting. Rifles.

Decoration. Flintlock. HUNTING. Rifles.

Decoration. Flintlock. Hunting. RIFLES.

b) Cycling produces as many entries as there are elements; in addition, references from synonyms and the names of related classes would have to be made. It produces a specific entry under each element but, like rotation, does not juxtapose elements; for example, the enquirer looking for information on the decoration of rifles would not find all documents easily. Unlike rotation, cycling maintains the same order of elements in each entry.

Cycling may be used in alphabetical subject catalogues; in classified catalogues, provided that the notation is expressive; and in alphabetical subject indexes.

c) Combination indexing; KWIC; Permutation indexing; Rotation; Shunting

D

DECIMAL NOTATION

a) Fractional notation using a base of 10, so that there are ten notational divisions available at every step.

DECREASING CONCRETENESS

a) A guide in the choice of citation order: the more concrete facet—or the more concrete name in an alphabetical subject heading—should be cited first; eg Maps—Cataloguing.

c) PMEST; Standard citation order.

DECREASING GENERALITY see GRADATION IN SPECIALITY

DEFINITION

a) One of Aristotle's original five predicables: the relationship

45

between a predicate and a subject such that the predicate states the essential nature of the subject; as in 'Firearms are *projectile weapons whose propellant is an explosive charge.*'

c) Attribute; Difference; Predicates; Species.

DENOTATION

a) The set of class members implied by a term; eg the class labelled Rifles has the denotation 'all firearms with spirally grooved bores intended to spin the bullet'.

c) Connotation; Extension.

DEPENDENCE

a) A guide in choosing citation order: if one of two elements could not exist without the other, then it should be cited after that other; eg, a document entitled *The decoration of firearms* should, by this principle, be collocated with other works on firearms, not with other works on decoration—you can't decorate something which isn't there!

c) Context dependency; Gradation by speciality; Standard citation order.

DEPENDENT FACETS *see* SUBFACETS

DEPENDENT WORKS

a) Those which cannot be used without some other previously produced work—eg indexes, concordances.

c) Related works.

DEPTH INDEXING

a) The indexing of subthemes in a document, as opposed to summarisation; eg, to index a work for which Phobias could be used as a specific summarisation under terms such as Claustrophobia, Agoraphobia, School phobia etc.

b) Depth indexing increases recall performance for the subthemes, but is likely to decrease precision.

c) Analytical entries; Exhaustive indexing; Exhaustivity; Partitioning; Polytopical work.

DESCRIPTIVE CATALOGUING

a) That part of the indexing process which is concerned to

identify and characterise a document, by the recording of information such as title, author's name, edition, imprint details, collation and membership of a series.

c) Enrichment; Limited cataloguing; Notes.

DESCRIPTORS

a) Representations of a document's subject under which records of the document are found in an index; eg, preferred synonyms in a Uniterm index, notational symbols in a classified catalogue.

b) Mooers, who coined the term, gives a more restricted meaning: a descriptor is an index term (ie a term under which records are to be made) together with a definition—and the definition is the more important: any label may be used, provided it is adequately defined for the indexing system.

c) Accessibility measure; Entry vocabulary; Index vocabulary; Specifiers.

DESIGNATIONS

a) Statements of the nature of the contribution made to a work, in an author-type heading; eg, Hope, David, *translator*; Smith, F, *editor*.

DEVELOPMENTAL ORDER *see* CHRONOLOGICAL ORDER

DICTIONARY CATALOGUE

a) A combined author/title and alphabetical pre-coordinate subject catalogue, (usually an alphabetico-direct subject catalogue).

c) Divided catalogue; Syndetic structure.

DIFFERENCE

a) One of the five predicables: that which distinguishes one species of a genus from others—eg *motorised* canoes; *timber* churches; *flintlock* firearms; *aestivating* dragons (ie dragons which are dormant in summer, to avoid the danger of spontaneous combustion).

b) Most classification schemes fail to provide for a concept as both a focus and a difference, so that it is not possible to differentiate between *timber for churches* and *timber churches*;

between *aestivation of dragons* (which is about aestivation) and *aestivating dragons* (which is about a kind of dragon, and need not discuss aestivation at all). LEC2 provides an example of a scheme which does; eg Backwardness in adolescence has the notation RedJbm, but Backward adolescents the notation TikRed.

c) Characteristic of division; Logical division; Superimposed class.

DIFFERENTIAL FACET

a) A facet in which some foci may only be cited when certain other foci are present.

b) Consider a classification scheme for arms and armour: there will be, among others, a Weapons facet (with foci such as Swords, Staff weapons, Missile weapons, Firearms . . .) and a Parts facet (Hilts, Blades, Barrels, Triggers . . .); but not all foci in the Parts facet will be applicable to all foci in the Weapons facet—swords do not have triggers, and guns do not have blades. The Parts facet is therefore a differential facet.

DIFFUSE AUTHORSHIP

a) A condition of authorship in which so many persons are involved that author entry becomes unimportant, the work usually being cited by title.

DIRECT ACCESS

a) Access to a computer store which does not involve a computerised scan through all the records held in the store.

c) On-line access; Sequential access.

DIRECT CODING

a) In item entry systems, the use of one hole per concept; the example shows an edge-notched card used to code a library school student's choices for LA second year papers—in this case, papers A2 and B13.

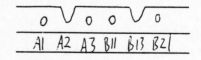

b) Direct coding is fast, both to code and to search, and false drops are avoided; but it restricts the number of concepts which can be encoded for a collection of documents to the number of holes available; eg 75 or 128 on edge-notched cards.

c) Indirect coding.

DIRECT ENTRY

a) Entry under headings which are in ordinary language order; eg Domestic architecture as opposed to Architecture, domestic.

c) Alphabetico-classed catalogue; Alphabetico-direct catalogue; Structured headings.

DISCIPLINARY CLASSIFICATION SCHEMES see ASPECT CLASSIFICATION SCHEMES

DISJUNCTION see LOGICAL SUM

DISPLAY

a) The second line of a PRECIS entry, containing the concepts which depend upon the lead term; eg 'Cataloguing', in

Maps. University libraries.
Cataloguing.

c) Qualifier.

DISTINCT SUBJECTS

a) Named subjects (as opposed to subjects which can only be identified by descriptive phrases), which should according to Cutter be given specific entry in an alphabetical subject catalogue.

c) Established subjects; Indistinct subjects.

DISTRIBUTED RELATIVES

a) Those classes whose documents are scattered on systematically ordered shelves or in single entry systematic catalogues because of the choice of citation order; eg, the citation order Persons taught-Subject taught-Teaching method results in very severe separation of works on, say, Team teaching; less severe scattering of works on Mathematics; and collocation of works on Secondary schoolchildren.

c) Chain procedure; Multiple entry indexing systems; Primary facet; Relative index.

DIVIDED CATALOGUES
a) Catalogues may be divided either to reduce the bulk of a sequence, and so make the catalogue easier to use, or to help the user to structure his approach (of course, some forms of catalogue are necessarily divided, because the headings do not interfile—the classified catalogue—or because headings for one section do not exist—item entry post-coordinate systems).

b) Catalogues may be divided by form of material, giving separate catalogues for books, for films, for recordings; or by arrangement, breaking a dictionary catalogue down into an author/title/series catalogue and an alphabetico-direct subject catalogue.

DOCUMENT SURROGATES *see* DUMMT BOOKS; SURROGATES

DOCUMENTS
a) Generic term for the information-bearing media handled by librarians—books, serials, sound recordings, films, illustrations etc.

c) Bibliographic unit; Physical form of documents.

DOUBLE DICTIONARY *see* DUAL DICTIONARY

DOUBLE-KWIC
a) A combination of KWIC and KWOC indexing: all entries under a KWOC heading are rotated in KWIC fashion, so that each pair of terms is brought together; eg, for a document entitled *Play therapy for maladjusted children* the following entries would be made:

Children
    maladjusted children/   Play therapy for
    Play therapy for maladjusted children/
    therapy for maladjusted children/   Play
Maladjusted
    children/   Play therapy for maladjusted
    Play therapy for maladjusted children/
    therapy for maladjusted children/   Play
etc.

c) Paired keyword indexing.

DOWNWARD REFERENCES

a) 'See also' references made from a superordinate to a subordinate class, to enable searches to be narrowed; eg Mental illness *see also* Schizophrenia.

b) Such references should modulate, for efficient searching; eg, Diseases *see also* Mental illness; Mental illness *see also* Schizophrenia, rather than Diseases *see also* Schizophrenia.

c) Bypassing references; Chain; Horizontal references; Upward references.

DUAL DICTIONARIES

a) Two Uniterm indexes to the same collection bound together in book-form, with several entries per page.

b) Dual dictionaries facilitate comparison of different entries to discover accession numbers common to both; there are no cards to remove or insert after use; and a number of copies may be made, so that one user does not prevent other people from using the index.

DUMMY BOOKS

a) Placed on shelves to remind users of material in other sequences or on loan.

b) This solution to the problem of parallel sequences seems wasteful of space and effort, and unnecessary—enquirers would do better to rely on the catalogue to correct this kind of separation.

E

EDGE-NOTCHED CARDS

a) Cards for item-entry post-coordinate indexing, with one or two rows of holes along each edge, which represent concepts; concepts are encoded by clipping open appropriate holes, so that when a rod is passed through those holes through the whole pack, required cards fall off. See illustration on p. 52.

c) Aperture cards; Coding; False drops; Punched cards.

EDITION
    a) All the copies of a book produced from one setting of type.
    b) A new edition provides opportunity for changes in the text—

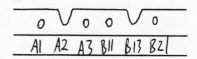

but does not imply that changes have in fact been made—so that the edition statement is an important part of the description of a book.
    c) Facsimile reprint; Impression; Issue; Reprint.

EDITOR
    a) 'One who prepares for publication a work or collection of works not his own'.—ICCP.
    b) The extent of an editor's contribution may vary from mere preparation of the manuscript for publication to choice of author, control of his work, and shaping of the final product.
    c) Editorial direction.

EDITORIAL DIRECTION
    a) Implies that the contributors to a composite work have worked under strong editorial control.
    b) The difference between a work produced under editorial direction and an edited collection was formerly important in AACR; in early 1975 it seems that the distinction may be abandoned.

EDUCATIONAL AND SCIENTIFIC CONSENSUS
    a) Bliss's term for the view of the structure of knowledge generally held by educated people, which should guide the classificationist in making his scheme.
    c) Consensus.

EMPTY DIGITS
    a) Notational symbols which do not represent concepts but have a structural role; for example, facet indicators, repeater digits in sector notation, and fence notation.

END PRODUCT *see* PURPOSE

ENERGY

a) One of Ranganathan's fundamental categories: that to which facets containing concepts of action and, in editions of CC up to X CC6, concepts of Problems, Properties and Processes are assigned; eg foci in the Energy facet of Zoology in CC includes what zoologists *do*—collecting, staining, classification—and also what happens in organisms—metabolism, transpiration, fatigue etc. Energy facets come third in the citation order represented by PMEST.

ENRICHED KEYWORD INDEXES

a) Keyword indexes supplemented by terms added by the indexer to provide helpful access points. An extreme example is provided by the article entitled *On the construction and care of white elephants*, which would presumably receive only one entry in a KWIC index:

e of white elephants/   [Catalogues] On the construction and ca

b) As all documents must be scanned if enriched keyword indexing is used, much of the economy of uncontrolled indexing disappears.

ENRICHMENT

a) Information in the 'collation statement' for a non-book medium which does not tell the enquirer what sort of equipment is necessary, nor the extent of the document, but does add something to the characterisation; eg, whether a microscope slide is stained, whether a film is in colour, whether a sound tape is Dolby processed (LANCET).

ENTITIES

a) Things, as opposed to the properties of and actions on and of things; eg Owls as opposed to Respiration; Pistols as opposed to Testing; Sword blades as opposed to Shape.

b) The proposed CRG general classification scheme, following the work of Barbara Kyle, was to have two main facets: Entities and Attributes.

ENTRIES

a) The records generated by documents in catalogues and

53

indexes.

b) Traditionally entries have been distinguished from refer
ences—that is, entries has been taken to mean descriptions o
documents in catalogues and indexes; but following ICCP a
records placed in the catalogue as the result of the acquisition of a
document are called entries.

c) Added entries; Alternative entry; Analytical entries; Head
ings; Main entries; Open entry; Unit entry.

ENTRY TERMS

a) The terms in an index vocabulary under which no document
are to be entered, but which merely guide the enquirer to the de
scriptors; eg, synonyms from which references are made (Teen
agers *see* Adolescents), or terms which are replaced by semanti
factors (Fathers *use* Male + Parents).

c) Specifiers.

ENTRY VOCABULARY *see* ENTRY TERMS

ENTRY WORD

a) The word which determines the primary filing position of ar
item.

ENUMERATIVE CLASSIFICATION SCHEMES

a) Those which attempt to enumerate—list—composite and
superimposed classes, as well as simple classes.

b) The traditional classification schemes—DC, LC, BC—are
basically enumerative (although most schemes have some degree
of synthesis). As a result they are bulky, tend to be inflexible, are di
 fficult to update, and fail to provide for many classes (eg DC 18 stil
has no provision for the class Gothic churches; in DC 17 it was pos
sible to specify Wines (641.872), Beers (641.873) and Spirits
(641.874), but not the class Alcoholic beverages: it is easier to
make this sort of error in constructing enumerative schemes be
cause of their greater complexity).

c) Faceted classification schemes.

ESTABLISHED SUBJECTS

a) Those which have been accepted as distinct and viable by a
society. (Consider the status of Statistics, Cybernetics, Information

54

etrieval, Psephology . . .).

b) For indexers the concept is probably not very useful: if there is literary warrant for a concept it is of no concern to the indexer whether or not it is 'established'.

c) Distinct subjects; Indistinct subjects.

EULER CIRCLES

a) Diagrammatic representations of class inclusion, eg

c) Venn diagrams.

EVOLUTIONARY ORDER *see* CHRONOLOGICAL ORDER

EXCLUSION *see* CONDITIONAL EXCLUSION; LOGICAL DIFFERENCE

EXHAUSTIVE INDEXING

a) Very detailed depth indexing.

c) Exhaustivity; Specificity.

EXHAUSTIVITY

a) The degree to which depth indexing is practised. To index a document entitled *Weapons* under terms such as Swords, Firearms, Staff weapons would be to index with less exhaustivity than if one used index terms such as Blades, Hilts, Triggers etc.

b) Greater exhaustivity increases recall performance at the expense of precision.

EXPOSITION PHASE

a) A phase relationship in which one phase is explained, or

explored, in terms of the other; eg, a Marxist interpretation of the novels of the Brontës; an ethological explanation of man's aggression.

EXPRESSIVE NOTATION

a) Notation which displays its synthetic structure; eg

RavMenLep (Group teaching of foreign languages in primary schools, synthesised from Rav—Primary schools; Men—foreign languages; Lep—Group teaching from LEC1).

820–31"18" (English nineteenth century novel, synthesised from 820—English literature;—31—Novels; '18'—nineteenth century; from UDC).

b) Expressiveness prevents the same notation being used for a synthetic and an enumerated class; preserves the required filing order; and may allow the same digit to be used in different facets with different meanings—eg, in the notation ND,11;5:5 (Casting bronze equestrian figures, from CC) ;5 = Bronze, but :5 = Casting.

c) Facet indicators; Fence notation; Hierarchical notation; Retroactive notation; Structural notation.

EXTENSION

a) The size of the set of members of a class; eg the extension of the class Firearms is greater than that of the class Rifles; the extension of the class Children is greater than that of the class Maladjusted children.

b) The extension of a class varies inversely with its intension (2).

c) Broader-narrower order; Connotation; Denotation; Genus-species relationship.

EXTENSION DEVICE *see* VERBAL EXTENSION

F

FACET

a) The set of simple classes which have the same relationship to the universe which is the subject of classification, because they all share a characteristic not shared by other sets.

b) Suppose the universe were Librarianship: the classi-ficationist might derive the following facets from an examination of the literature—Libraries facet (all the simple classes are kinds of library); Materials facet (all the simple classes are kinds of library material); Operations facet (what librarians do: management, selection, indexing, making tea etc). Similarly, if the universe were Social welfare, facets such as Persons (children, librarians, females etc), Problems (deafness, poverty, maladjustment etc) and Thera-pies (guaranteed minimum income, aversion therapy, surgery, slum clearance etc) would be discovered.

c) Common facets; Faceted classification schemes; Foci; Fun-damental categories; Subfacets.

FACET ANALYSIS

a) The process of recognising facets which is the basis of the construction of faceted classification schemes.

b) In special classification schemes it is usual to apply facet analysis to the universe which is the subject of classification; the only general faceted classification scheme yet pub-lished—CC—first divides the universe—in this case, the whole of knowledge—into conventional areas (main classes, canonical classes) within which facet analysis is applied. However, the pro-posed CRG general scheme will apply the technique to the whole of knowledge, producing two great facets of Entities and Attributes.

FACET FORMULA

a) The statement of citation order; eg Thing-Part-Material; PMEST.

FACET INDICATORS

a) Introductory symbols peculiar to each facet which make the notation expressive; eg RavMenLep (from LEC1, which uses capital letters as facet indicators), ND,18;5:5 (from CC, which uses punc-tuation marks as facet indicators).

c) Arbitrary symbols; Fence notation; retroactive notation.

FACET SEPARATORS see FENCE NOTATION

FACETED CLASSIFICATION SCHEMES

a) Schemes in which simple classes only are enumerated, arranged in facets. Superimposed and composite classes are expressed by synthesised notation constructed by the indexer.

b) The theory of faceted classification schemes was worked ou
by Ranganathan, and exemplified in his CC; the efficiency, econ
omy, simplicity and flexibility of such schemes has made them
popular for librarians wishing to construct special schemes, and (i
early 1975) two more general schemes based on facet analysis ar
at some stage of production—the CRG general scheme and the
new edition of BC.

c) Enumerative classification schemes.

FACSIMILE REPRINTS

a) Replicas of previously produced books, usually printed by
photo-lithography.

b) Such reprints are best treated as new publications when they
have new title-pages; although, of course, notes about the origina
publication must be made.

c) Impression.

FALSE COORDINATIONS see FALSE DROPS

FALSE DROPS

a) Irrelevant documents displayed to the searcher in a post-
coordinate indexing system. The term derives from edge-notched
cards, but it is used by analogy in connection with other post-
coordinate index forms, and even in connection with pre-
coordinate systems.

b) False drops may be caused by human error in indexing or
searching; by the use of uncontrolled index vocabularies, so that
homographs are not distinguished; by the use of certain coding
systems (7–4–2–1, Binary coding, Superimposed random
coding); and above all by the failure of simple post-coordinate
systems to show the nature of relationship between index terms—
for example, is a document indexed under the three terms Children,
Death and Parents about the effect on children of the death of
parents; the effect on parents of children's deaths; or about how
parents deal with a child's questions about death?

c) Links; Qualifiers; Roles; Thesauri; Weighting.

FALSE LINKS

a) In chain procedure: a class which is apparently part of a chain, but is in fact not.

   b) False links result from

1) notation which is only apparently hierarchical; eg

600	Technology
620	Engineering
621	Mechanical
621.3	Electrical

when indexing a work on electrical engineering, the false link
Mechanical engineering should not be indexed);

2) the use of 'portmanteau' classes, which either reflect out-of-date
relationships; eg

598	Reptiles and birds
598.2	Birds
598.91	Birds of prey

there is no point in indexing Reptiles and birds for a work on birds
of prey) or are merely intended to indicate the scope of a class; eg

380.5	Transportation services
387	Water, air and space transport
387.7	Air transport

no point in indexing Water, air and space transport for a work on air
transport);

3) errors of subordination by the maker of the scheme; eg

788	Wind musical instruments
788.1/.48	Brass
788.43	Saxophone

when indexing a work on the saxophone, an entry under Brass
instruments would be unhelpful—the saxophone is not a brass
instrument).

   c) Hidden links; Unsought links.

FAVOURED CATEGORY
   a) A class placed at the beginning of a sequence instead of in its
logical position, because of local interest; eg, in western countries,
placing Christianity before any other religion; in English-speaking
countries, placing English language and literature before any other.

   c) Bias; Critical indexing.

FEATURE CARDS see OPTICAL COINCIDENCE CARDS

FEATURE HEADINGS
   a) In a classified file: a translation of notation into ordinary lan-

guage, as a guide for the searcher; eg RavMenLep—Primary schools. Foreign languages. Group teaching.

b) An alternative format, used in BNB until recently, is to provide a 'pyramid' of steps of division:

Rav—Primary schools
    Men—Foreign languages
        Lep—Group teaching

Feature headings may also be used to correct unhelpful separation by references; eg 655.4—Publishing *see also* 658.809 001 552—Bookselling.

c) Connective index entries; Guiding; Verbal extensions.

FENCE NOTATION

a) Notation made expressive by the use of a separating symbol which marks off one facet from another in synthetic notation; eg DGWE/BL. If pure notation is required the first digit in the series is reserved as the fence (in order for synthetic notation to file correctly, the fence must have a filing value less than that of any notation for concepts); eg DGWEABL.

b) Fence notation preserves the required filing order, and differentiates synthetic from enumerated notation—eg, the difference between DGWEBL and DGWE/BL is clear; but does not release notation for use in other facets unless the fence is repeated, as in the first three editions of CC.

c) Facet indicators; Retroactive notation.

FIELDS (1)

a) The sets of holes on item entry cards, each of which is used to encode one concept.

c) Fixed field coding systems; Superimposed random coding.

FIELDS (2)

a) Discrete areas on computer input media reserved for particular types of information—eg author field, in which authors' names are recorded; title field, edition field etc.

c) Fixed fields; Tags; Variable fields.

FILE ORGANISATION

a) The basis for the arrangement of entries in a catalogue, index

r computer store; eg systematic (as in a classified catalogue); term
ntry (as with optical coincidence cards).

b) Choice of file organisation does not seem to affect recall and
recision performance, but other factors such as ease of con-
truction, ease of use and cost may vary.

c) Inverted files; Item entry; Physical forms of catalogue; Unin-
erted files.

ILIATORY ORDER

a) The order of classes in generic relationships.

b) Genus-species relationship.

ILING ORDER (1)

a) The order in which documents or records of documents file,
s a result of the application of a classification scheme.

b) Note that this order is not necessarily the same as schedule
rder—the order in which classes appear on the pages of the
cheme; for example, in CC the facets appear on the page in the
ame order as the facet forumla, but of course the filing order,
naintained by facet indicators, is the reverse.

c) Arbitrary symbols; Broader-narrower order; Inversion; Sche-
lule order; Shelf order.

FILING ORDER (2)

a) The relative position of items in an alphabetical sequence.

c) Letter by letter; Word by word.

FINDING LIST CATALOGUES

a) Catalogues which enable the searcher easily to discover
vhether a particular required document is available, at the expense
of the catalogue's bibliographic function; eg, by entering works
under the name of the author which appears on the title-page
ather than under a uniform heading.

c) Bibliographic catalogues (1).

FIVE PREDICABLES see PREDICABLES

FIXED FIELD CODING SYSTEMS

a) Indirect coding systems for edge notched cards which allow
only one digit to be encoded in each field for a document, to avoid,

or reduce the number of, false drops. This restricts the number of terms which can be encoded for documents.

c) 7—4—2—1 coding; 7—4—2—1—S—0 coding; Binary coding; Pyramid coding; Superimposed random coding.

FIXED FIELDS

a) Computer input fields of a fixed length—allowing a fixed number of characters for each type of information, which cannot be exceeded.

b) Fixed fields simplify programing, because tags do not need to be added to 'tell' the computer what sort of information is being input—it will 'know' from character counts that a new field has begun. On the other hand, information may have to be abbreviated to fit into the alloted length—eg an unusually long author's name may have to be cut short.

c) Variable fields.

FIXED LOCATION

a) Locating documents by their positions relative to a shelf.

b) Fixed location saves space and makes shelving easier—there is no need to leave spaces at the ends of shelves to allow for insertion of new accessions, and shelf marks are likely to be simple. On the other hand, because insertion within the sequence is not practical systematic order is not possible, and browsing becomes difficult; fixed location is therefore usually used in closed access or completed collections.

c) Relative location; Sequential location.

FLEXIBILITY (1)

a) The ability of a classification scheme to allow alternative locations for a subject, to suit local needs.

b) Flexibility may be achieved by reserving alternative notations for the same subject (eg BC allows Religion to be placed in the Social sciences at P, or with Philosophy at A)—but note that this wastes notation: a library must choose one alternative, and this leaves the other notations permanently unused; or provision for changing citation order may be made (requiring facet indicators in the form of arbitrary symbols if broader-narrower filing order is to be maintained with every possible citation order).

FLEXIBILITY (2)

a) A quality of physical forms of catalogue: the ease with which new entries may be inserted and obsolete entries removed.

b) Flexibility is greatest in the card catalogue, and, at the other extreme, impossible in the bound printed book form.

FOCI (singular: Focus)

a) The elemental classes produced by the application of characteristics of division, whose sum is the facet.

b) For example, the Library operations facet of a classification scheme on Librarianship will consist of foci such as Document selection, Document organisation, Exploitation of stock, Management etc; the Parts facet of a classification scheme on Weapons will consist of foci such as Barrels, Triggers, Hilts; the Persons facet of a classification scheme on Social welfare will consist of foci such as Children, Old people, Males, Females, Immigrants, Librarians etc.

c) Isolates; Simple classes; Subfacets.

FORM CLASSES

a) In a classification scheme, those classes in which bibliographic or literary form is preferred to subject as the basis for arrangement.

b) Literary texts provide an example: the fact that *Troilus and Criseyde* and *Troilus and Cressida* are obviously on the same subject is insignificant compared to the fact that one is an English poem by Chaucer and the other an English play by Shakespeare and in the class Literature the citation order for texts is likely to be Language-Form-Period, omitting subject entirely. Generalia classes are also an example of form class: here, subject matter is so diffuse that arrangement can only be by bibliographic form.

FORM FACETS *see* COMMON FACETS

FORM SUBHEADINGS (1)

a) In alphabetical subject catalogues, names of literary and bibliographic forms used as subheadings; eg Firearms—Dictionaries.

FORM SUBHEADING (2)

a) In author/title cataloguing, the use of forms as subheadings;

especially common with corporate authors; eg Australia. *Constitution*; Catholic Church. *Liturgy and ritual*.

FORMS *see* FORMS OF PRESENTATION; PHYSICAL FORMS OF CATALOGUE: PHYSICAL FORMS OF DOCUMENT

FORMS OF PRESENTATION
a) The forms in which information is presented in documents, as opposed to the physical forms of the documents themselves; eg a dictionary of architecture; an encyclopaedia of arms and armour; essays on art.

b) Citation order is usually Subject-Form, although this may be changed for particular local purposes—eg it might be helpful to keep all bibliographies together, close to the library catalogue. It may be difficult to differentiate a form of presentation from a physical form; for example, a map is a method of presenting information but usually also provides storage problems because of its physical form; the physical form and form of presentation of serials are inextricable. Perhaps the important distinction is that forms of presentation are the province of the indexer; physical forms are a management rather than an intellectual problem.

FRACTIONAL NOTATION
a) Notation which is divisible, to allow for the insertion of new classes in the correct place—that is, to be hospitable. Thus, the new class Wheellock firearms may be inserted in the following sequence between Matchlocks and Flintlocks by giving it the notation GBDE:
GBD Matchlock firearms
GBE Flintlock firearms
GBF Percussion cap firearms
c) Arithmetical notation; Decimal notation; Gap notation.

FREE INDEXING
a) Indexing in which the indexer chooses terms from the document or from his own knowledge, without the use of ready-prepared index vocabularies.
c) Concept indexing; Natural language indexing.

64

FUNDAMENTAL CATEGORIES

a) Generalised facets, or basic *types* of classes, to one of which any facet or any class may be assigned; eg Kaiser's Concretes—Processes; the CRG's general classification scheme's Entities—Attributes; Ranganthan's PMEST.

FUNDAMENTAL CLASS

a) The context from which a concept can never be divorced, however many other contexts it may appear in; eg, Horses may appear in Agriculture, Sport, War, Transport etc, but its fundamental class is Biology; Coal may appear in Economics, Mining, Fuel technology etc, but its fundamental class is Geology.

b) In an aspect classification scheme the fundamental class may be used to take general works on the subject, covering all aspects. In a grouped alphabetical subject index the fundamental class provides the least-limiting subheading; eg

Horses
  Fundamental class
    Zoology   599.725
  Use aspects
    Circuses   791.32
    Racing   798.4
  Technical aspects
    Breaking   636.108 81
    Breeding   636.108 2
  Transcendental aspects
  in Art   704.943 2

In the CRG general classification scheme, entities would be placed in their rank in the sequence of integrative levels according to the concept of fundamental class.

c) Uniquely defining class

G

GAP NOTATION

a) Arithmetical notation with some symbols left unused in attempt to achieve hospitality; eg
Mab Matchlock guns
Mac Flintlock guns

Mad

Mae

Maf Percussion cap guns

b) Gap notation is used in LC (and in the Cheltenham Classification, devised by the librarians of Cheltenham Ladies' College). It does not achieve absolute hospitality, because gaps get filled; and it does not achieve true hospitality even when gaps are available, because they are likely to be in the wrong place; for example, the classes Snaphaunce guns and Wheellock guns ought to file between Matchlock and Flintlock guns, but will have to use the notations Mad and Mae so that the order in array suffers.

c) Fractional notation.

GENERAL CLASS *see* GENERALIA CLASS

GENERAL CLASSIFICATION SCHEMES

a) Those which cover, or attempt to cover, the whole of knowledge.

c) Special classification schemes.

GENERAL-SPECIAL ORDER

a) A kind of broader-narrower order, in which no document on a species of a genus files before works on the genus; eg, the class Gothic churches does not file before the class Churches.

c) Helpful order; Inversion.

GENERAL SUBJECTS

a) In J D Brown's SC, the aspects of concretes: the standpoints from which concretes may be viewed; eg church *architecture; geology* of coal; flower *gardening.*

b) In SC the citation order is Concretes-General subjects, which is the reverse of that found in aspect classification schemes.

GENERAL SYSTEMS THEORY

a) A classification of systems which places them in an order of increasing complexity.

c) Integrative levels.

GENERALIA CLASS

a) A main class in a general classification scheme which takes works whose subjects cover too much area to allow them to be placed in any subject main class—eg, general encyclopaedias.

b) A true generalia class is a form class—the only basis for arrangement is the form of presentation or physical form of the documents; it is significant that in CC the contents of the generalia class are the same as the list of common isolates. However, many schemes include subject classes in their generalia class; eg DC includes Librarianship and Journalism in this class.

GENERALITY *see* GRADATION IN SPECIALITY

GENERIC ENTRY

a) Entry made under a broader class than that of the document; eg, entering a work on Rifles under the term Firearms in a Uniterm index.

b) Generic entry increases recall performance at the expense of precision.

c) Broad classification; Punch also.

GENERIC POSTING *see* GENERIC ENTRY

GENERIC RELATIONSHIPS

a) The relationships between superordinate, subordinate, co-ordinate and collateral classes; between a thing and its kind, and between the kinds of a thing.

c) Hierarchy.

GENERIC SEARCH

a) A search for all documents on a subject, including those on its subdivisions.

b) In systematic catalogues generic searches are facilitated by collocation; in alphabetical subject catalogues references are used (eg Mental illness *see also* Schizophrenia); in post-coordinate systems references in the index or a structured index vocabulary are used.

GENUS

a) One of the five predicables: a class capable of subdivision into species, which are kinds of the thing represented by the class.

c) Difference; Logical division.

GENUS-SPECIES RELATIONSHIP
a) The relationship between a thing and its kinds; eg between Dogs and Spaniels, Greyhounds, Yorkshire terriers etc.

c) General-special order; Species; Syntagmatic relationships.

GRADATION IN SPECIALITY
a) Bliss's principle for the order of main classes, based upon the premise that sciences and other subjects of study may be regarded as relatively more or less general; one indication of this is that 'the generalisations and laws of each more general science are true in some measure of all the more special sciences'—eg Physics is more general than Biology, because Physics is the science of matter in general, while Biology deals only with living matter; and because while Biology may use concepts from Physics, Physics does not use concepts from Biology. On this basis, classes may be placed in an order of decreasing generality, or gradation in speciality.

c) Dependence.

GROUP NOTATION
a) The extension of the base for coordinate classes in a hierarchical notation by using two (or more) digits instead of one. With two numbers, say, 90 class numbers can look coordinate; with only one number, only 10 class numbers can look coordinate.

b) UDC's centesimal notation provides an example; eg

354	Ministries (ie departments of central government)
354.11	Foreign office
354.12	Colonial office
354.13	Commonwealth relations, etc, down to
354.86	Food

in all 25 classes which are coordinate and which look coordinate; compare this with the situation if group notation were not used:

354	Ministries
354.1	Foreign Office
354.2	Colonial office
354.3	Commonwealth relations, etc, down to
354.24	Insurance
354.25	Food

when the Ministry of Food would not look coordinate with, say, the

Foreign Office.
   c) Sector notation.

GROUPED ALPHABETICAL SUBJECT INDEX
   a) Metcalfe's attack on the illogicality of straight alphabetical order in the conventional index prompted Coates to suggest a grouping of entries, at least for large collections (Coates suggests over 100,000 items); eg
Weapons
   Fundamental class
        Engineering   623.4
   Use aspects
        Ceremonial   394
        Hunting   799
        War   355
   Technical aspects
        Manufacture   623.4
   Transcendental aspects
        Collecting   739.7
        Customs   399
        Folklore   398.362
   c) Chain procedure; Fundamental class; Uniquely defining class.

GROUPED HEADINGS
   a) In dictionary catalogues and name catalogues it is usual to sub-arrange entries with the same heading by type; eg, into an author sequence, a subject sequence and a title sequence—
Dickens, Charles
   Bleak House
Dickens, Charles
   Tale of two cities
Dickens, Charles
   Foster, John
      Life of Charles Dickens
   c) Name catalogues.

GROUPED SUBHEADINGS
   a) In alphabetical subject catalogues it is usual to group sub-headings by type; eg, into a form sequence, a place sequence, a

subdivision sequence and an inverted form sequence—
Architecture
Architecture—Dictionaries
Architecture—Periodicals
Architecture—Great Britain
Architecture—USA
Architecture—Design
Architecture—Practice
Architecture, Domestic
Architecture, Military

GROUPING *see* COLLOCATION

GUARDBOOK CATALOGUES
   a) Catalogues made by the scrap-book process of sticking entries onto the pages of a bound or loose-leaf book. Used at the BM; to be discontinued, one hopes, now that it has become the BL.
   b) This form allows flexibility through the laborious process of unsticking and re-arranging entries. It produces a bulky catalogue.
   c) Book form catalogues; Printed catalogues.

GUIDING
   a) To display the structure of an ordered sequence of items by the use of labels (on catalogues, and on bays, presses and shelves housing documents); feature headings (in classified catalogues); tabs of different cut (in card catalogues); typography and layout (in book form catalogues) etc.

H

HEADINGS
   a) Terms which determine the filing position of entries in a catalogue; these may be names of authors (author headings), titles of documents, series titles, names of editors etc; and descriptors—that is, subject statements used as headings.

HELPFUL ORDER
   a) An order of items which itself guides the user to related items,

and helps him to extend, broaden and narrow his search.
   c) Broader-narrower order; Order in array; Systematic order

HEURISTIC SEARCHES
   a) Searches whose strategy is, or may be, continually modified as results of the search appear.
   c) Browsing; Iterative searches.

HIDDEN LINKS
   a) A class which is part of a chain, and which should be indexed by chain procedure when a narrower class is indexed, but which may be overlooked because the notation is not hierarchical; eg, the classes Biology and Vertebrates in this chain for a work on mammals, taken from DC:

500 Science	
574	Biology
590	Zoological sciences
591	Zoology
592–599	Animals
596	Vertebrates
599	Mammals

   c) False links; Unsought links.

HIERARCHICAL NOTATION
   a) Notation which displays the relationship of subordination by its length; one digit being added for each step of division; eg (from CC):

D5	Vehicles
D51	Land
D515	Railway vehicles
D5153	Railway carriages
D51533	Passenger carriages
D515332	Higher class carriages
D515333	Lower class carriages
D52	Water vehicles
D525	Ships

   b) Hierarchical notation seems to be expected by library users, and it is certainly intellectually satisfying, besides making it easier to broaden and narrow searches; but it lengthens notation, and makes absolute hospitality impossible.

71

c) Expressive notation; Group notation; Ordinal notation; Sector notation; Structural notation.

HIERARCHICAL SEARCH *see* GENERIC SEARCH

HIERARCHY

a) A set of classes organised to display their generic relationships—of superordination, subordination, and the 'horizontal' relationships between collateral classes and between coordinate classes.

b) A hierarchy is often shown in diagrammatic form:

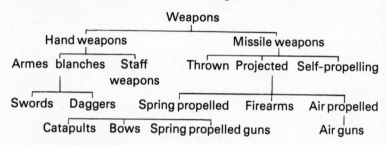

c) Logical division.

HOMOGRAPHS

a) Names for different concepts which happen to be spelled in the same way; eg

Alienation (a device in literature used by dramatists such as Brecht)
Alienation (mental illness)
Alienation (dissociation from society)
Alienation (symptom of emotional disturbance—failure to recognise familiar things)

b) Failure to control homographs leads to decreased precision.

c) Qualifiers; Roles; Synonyms.

HORIZONTAL REFERENCES

a) References made between collateral or coordinate classes; eg Firearms *see also* Air propelled missile weapons; Spring propelled guns *see also* Air guns (see diagram under HIERARCHY)

c) Downward references; Upward references.

HOSPITALITY

a) The ability to give a unique notational symbol to any class which is to be added to an existing classification scheme, which will correctly locate that class in relation to other classes. Hospitality to new simple classes is called 'hospitality in array'; hospitality to new superimposed or composite classes is called 'hospitality in chain'.

b) A classification scheme which uses gap notation is not truly hospitable; nor is a scheme which has a' class labelled 'other', to take any classes not thought of.

To be hospitable in array, notation must be fractional, and hierarchical notation must be abandoned if necessary—absolute hospitality with a hierarchical notation is not possible. To be hospitable in chain the scheme must be faceted, in addition to having a fractional and ordinal notation.

c) Arithmetical notation; Sector notation; Seminal mnemonics.

I

ISBN *see* International Standard Book Number

IDENTIFYING FACTORS

a) Those parts of the description of a document which, taken together, differentiate it from all other documents; for a printed book, for example, these include author's name, title of book, edition statement and imprint details.

c) Characterisation; Descriptive cataloguing.

IMPRESSION

a) Part of an edition: all copies of a book printed from the same setting of type at one time.

b) The wrapper of the 24th impression of John Le Carre's *Spy that came in from the cold* claimed it to be the 24th edition!

c) Facsimile reprint; Issue; Reprint.

INCLUSION *see* CLASS INCLUSION

INCREASING COMPLEXITY

a) A basis for order in array, in which the more complex class follows the less complex; eg, social groups arranged according to the complexity of their internal organisation.

c) General systems theory; Integrative levels; Size.

INDEX (1)

a) A list of terms in intelligible order, showing where in some other sequence further information may be found.

c) Alphabetical subject index; Chain procedure; PRECIS; Relative index; Specific index.

INDEX (2)

a) A tool which guides enquirers to the documents they require in a particular collection; a catalogue.

c) Post-coordinate indexing systems; Pre-coordinate indexing systems.

INDEX LANGUAGE

a) An indexing tool consisting of an index vocabulary together with rules for its use; eg, a classification scheme or a thesaurus.

c) Syntax.

INDEX TERMS *see* INDEX VOCABULARY

INDEX VOCABULARY

a) The set of terms—descriptors, specifiers and entry terms—which represent concepts in an index language.

b) Controlled index vocabularies; Natural language indexing; Structured index vocabularies; Syntax.

INDEXING (1)

a) Constructing an index (1).

INDEXING (2)

a) All the processes involved in organising stores of documents or stores of information: information retrieval.

INDIRECT CODING

a) In item entry indexing systems: using more than one hole for each concept to be coded.

b) Indirect coding is more economical in use of holes than is direct coding, because combinations of holes become available for use.

c) 7—4—2—1 coding; 7—4—2—1—S—0 coding; Binary coding; Fixed field coding systems; Pyramid coding; Superimposed random coding.

INDIRECT HEADINGS *see* ALPHABETICO-CLASSED CATALOGUES; STRUCTURED HEADINGS

INDISTINCT SUBJECTS

a) Subjects which have not acquired a name (as opposed to a descriptive phrase), and which, therefore, according to Cutter, cannot be given specific entry in an alphabetical subject catalogue.

b) Indistinct subjects are not a real problem to cataloguers who use an open-ended technique for the construction of subject headings, as advocated by Coates; they can always construct a specific heading.

c) Distinct subjects; Established subjects.

INFLUENCE PHASE RELATIONSHIP

a) The relationship between phases such that one influences the other; eg *The influence of C A Voysey on the English house*; *The effect of marxism on English literary criticism*.

INTEGER NOTATION *see* ARITHMETICAL NOTATION

INTEGRATIVE LEVELS

a) A biological idea which could provide an absolute basis for the order of entities in a classification scheme, replacing main classes as the backbone of classification schemes. The order is one of increasing complexity, reflecting the addition of properties, which results in levels of organisation; eg Physical entities (such as atoms, molecules); Chemical entities (such as compounds); Non-living matter (minerals, astronomic bodies); Living entities etc.

b) To be used as the basis of the proposed CGR general classification scheme.

c) General systems theory; Uniquely defining class.

INTEGRITY OF NUMBERS

a) The principle that the meaning of a piece of notation shall not be changed in future editions of a classification scheme.

    b)   Promised by Dewey for his DC, but abandoned in DC15.

    c)   Starvation.

INTELLECTUAL RESPONSIBILITY

    a)   A guide to the choice of main entry heading for an author/title catalogue: to make main entry under the person or corporate body primarily responsible for the content of the work.

    c)   Sought label.

INTENSION (1)

    a)   All the properties shared by the members of a class; eg, all Rifles are firearms with spirally grooved bores to spin the bullet; all have barrels and some form of stock; all include metal in their construction.

    c)   Connotation; Denotation; Subjective intension.

INTENSION (2)

    a)   The size of the set of properties which are essential to the definition of a class.

    b)   The intension of a class is in inverse proportion to its extension; eg Firearms has greater extension than Rifles, but less intension.

    c)   Broader-narrower order; Connotation; Genus-species relationship.

INTERDISCIPLINARY SUBJECTS

    a)   Those which cut across the boundaries of conventional disciplines—eg, conservation, biochemistry—and cause problems to the users of aspect classification schemes.

INTERFIXING *see* LINKS

INTERLINKING *see* INTERLOCKING DESCRIPTORS

INTERLOCKING DESCRIPTORS

    a)   The generic term used by Vickery for the linking devices—links and partitioning—used to increase precision in post-coordinate indexing systems.

INTERMEDIATE LEXICON

    a)   A list of terms representing concepts which appear in index vocabularies, which enables a translation from one vocabulary to another to be accomplished by matching the terms from the vocabularies which are to be reconciled with the term in the intermediate lexicon.

c) Microthesauri; Satellite thesauri

INTERNATIONAL STANDARD BOOK NUMBER

a) A number unique to a book, consisting of a set of digits representing the publisher, assigned by the Standard Book Numbering Agency; a title number, assigned by the publisher; and a check digit.

b) ISBNs result in economies in clerical work. Applications include LASER's location lists, which match ISBNs with holding libraries, and BNB's MARC tapes, whose entries are in ISBN order.

c) Accession numbers; Book numbers; Union catalogues.

INVERSION

a) If broader-narrower order on shelves or in a classified file is required, then the filing order of elements in synthetic notation must be the reverse of their citation order; this is called the principle of inversion.

b) Consider three documents entitled *Play therapy for the maladjusted, Play therapy for maladjusted children* and *Play therapy*. Whichever citation order we choose between the Therapy facet, the Problem facet and the Person facet, the broader-narrower order between these documents is Play therapy—Play therapy for the maladjusted—Play therapy for maladjusted children.

Suppose we choose the citation order Person-Problem-Therapy; the order of elements in the notations will be Play therapy; Maladjustment—Play therapy; and Children—Maladjustment—Play therapy. The notation assigned to Play therapy must therefore file before the notation assigned to Maladjustment, and the notation for Maladjustment must file before that of Children, if the required filing order between the documents is to be achieved; eg

B48   Play therapy
C21B48   Play therapy for the maladjusted
D35C21B48   Play therapy for maladjusted children
(B48—Play therapy—files before C21—Maladjustment—which files before D35—Children)

The same principle applies for the relationship between the citation order of superimposed classes and the filing order of subfacets.

INVERSION REFERENCES
a) 'See' references made to an alphabetical subject heading from the elements in reverse order, as used in BTI; eg
Noise: Rotors: Helicopters *see* Helicopters: Rotors: Noise.
Rotors: Helicopters *see* Helicopters: Rotors.
c) Chain procedure

INVERTED FILES
a) Computer files in which the information is held in term entry form; that is, documents are listed under descriptors—usually keywords.
c) Item entry; Uninverted files.

INVERTED HEADINGS *see* STRUCTURED HEADINGS

ISOLATES
a) Components of subjects which cannot themselves be regarded as subjects in Ranganathan's sense, because they may be studied in more than one discipline; for example, Coal is an isolate—it may be studied by experts in different disciplines, such as Economics, Fuel technology, Geology, Chemistry etc.
b) When isolates are attached to a basic class—to a particular discipline—they cease to be isolated, and become foci organised in facets.
c) Composite classes; Entity; Simple subjects; Subject (1); Superimposed classes.

ISSUE
a) Part of an edition or an impression; all copies of a book released at one time.
b) Sometimes issues are distinguished by different binding or different paper size; for example, a paperback version of a work produced from the same typesetting as the hardback version would be another issue.

ITEM ENTRY SYSTEMS
a) Post-coordinate indexing systems in which each card

represents a document, whose subject (or other access information) is encoded on the card by means of holes. The familiar forms are edge-notched cards and punched cards.

b) Item entry cards may be kept in random order; but the whole file must be searched to answer any request. As the cards may bear full information about the document (or even a copy of the document itself—eg in microform, or a photograph of a work of art), no supplementary index to accession numbers is necessary, as is often the case with term entry systems; but an index to the holes is necessary.

c) Coding; Partitioning; Term entry systems; Uninverted files.

ITEM ON TERM *see* TERM ENTRY SYSTEMS

ITEM TERM CARDS
a) An adaptation of item entry for use with punched cards: for each document one card is punched for each concept: that is, there are as many cards for each document as there are concepts to be indexed.

c) Although this greatly increases the size of the file it is more economical in use of holes than conventional punched card systems, because it enables superimposed random coding to be used.

ITERATIVE SEARCHING
a) Repeated searching, in which later searches are modified in the light of the results of earlier searches.

c) Heuristic searching.

J

JOIN *see* LOGICAL SUM

JOINT AUTHORSHIP
a) A work resulting from the collaboration of two or more authors whose contributions are not distinguishable from each other is a work of joint authorship.

c) Composite work.

K

KEYWORD

a) Significant term found in a document, in its title or in an abstract.

b) Keywords are the basis of natural language indexing systems.

c) Clumps; Double-KWIC; KWIC; KWOC; Normalised recall ratio: Whole text indexing.

KWAC *see* ENRICHED KEYWORD INDEXES

KWIC

a) KeyWord in Context—a multiple entry natural language indexing system, which retains the relative order of elements but brings the entry word to a constant filing position—usually in the centre of the page—with the rest of the terms 'wrapped round' it; so keeping the entry word 'in context'; eg, for a document entitled *Play therapy for maladjusted children*:

maladjusted	children/	Play therapy for
therapy for	maladjusted children/	Play
children/	Play therapy for maladjusted c
en/	Play	therapy for maladjusted childr

b) This system was discussed by Crestadoro in the mid-nineteenth century, and used by him at Manchester; but modern, computerised KWIC indexing derives from the work of Luhn in the 1950s. Insignificant terms are discovered by matching titles against a computer held stop list, which prevents their use as entry words, and the rotation is also performed by computer.

c) Double-KWIC; Enriched keyword indexing; KWOC; Rotation

KWOC

a) KeyWord Out of Context: an indexing system similar to KWIC, except that the entry word is used as a conventional heading, and very often not repeated in the title, being replaced by an

asterisk or some other symbol; eg
Children
    Play therapy for maladjusted *
Maladjusted
    Play therapy for * children
Play
    * therapy for maladjusted children
Therapy
    Play * for maladjusted children.
    b) This system gives a more conventional, and so more accept-
able, appearance to the index.
    c) Double-KWIC

L

LANGUAGE *see* CONTROLLED INDEX VOCABULARIES; INDEX
LANGUAGES; NATURAL LANGUAGE INDEXING SYSTEMS;
ORDINARY LANGUAGE; STRUCTURED INDEX VOCABULARIES

LEAD
    a) The entry word in a PRECIS entry; eg, 'maps' in
Maps. University libraries
    Cataloguing.
    c) Display; Qualifier.

LEAD IN TERM *see* ENTRY WORD

LEAP IN DIVISION *see* MODULATION

LENGTH *see* BREVITY

LETTER BY LETTER
    a) A filing method for headings in the form of words, in which
the letter is the filing unit; eg
    Eastbourne
    Easter Island
    Easte Row
    East Ham.

81

c) Word by word.

LEVELS

a) Facets in CC may be divided according to a number of characteristics; each of these is called a level of manifestation of the fundamental category to which the facet has been assigned. For example, in the class Botany the Personality facet has two subdivisions: Plants by species and Parts of plants. Plants by species is the first level manifestation of the Personality facet (written, in the facet formula, [P]; Parts of plants is the second level Personality facet (written in the facet formula, [P2].

b) In many cases, but not in all, levels seem to correspond to subfacets; eg, in Architecture, [P] and [P2] are buildings by place and style, and [P3] is buildings by use; but [P4] is Parts of buildings.

c) Rounds.

LEVELS OF INTEGRATION *see* INTEGRATIVE LEVELS

LIMITED CATALOGUING

a) Reduction in the detail of descriptive cataloguing—eg, omitting collation or imprint—or reduction of the number of entries made for a document, for economy or to make the catalogue less confusing for the inexperienced user.

b) Limited cataloguing usually reduces the value of the catalogue as a bibliographic tool; since the finding list function is basic, it cannot be allowed to suffer. However, limited cataloguing in the sense of a reduction in the number of entries may make searching more difficult.

c) Selective cataloguing; Union catalogues; Unit entry.

LINEAR SEQUENCE

a) An order of items in which one follows another, as books usually do on shelves.

b) Linear order is capable of showing one relationship only—that between the item and those which are next to it in the order. This limitation is overcome by the use of catalogues, in which multiple entry is practised. For example, it is not possible to place the same copy of H G Well's *Floor games* simultaneously with *The history of Mr Polly* and with other works on war games (one could buy two copies, but this is uneconomic in money and time, and inefficient in terms of indexing); but one may place two entries in the catalogue, one filed under the author's name, the other under the subject.

It is usually assumed that the shelf order of books must be a linear order, but in his televised series *America*, Alistair Cooke revealed that his books on American states are kept in a two-dimensional order for the convenience of his secretary. This order reflects the spatial relationships of states; for example, works on Tennessee would be immediately below those on Kentucky, immediately above those on Alabama, to the right of those on Arkansas and to the left of those on North Carolina.

LINK

a) A step in a chain, representing either a class or a relating device such as a facet indicator; eg, the following are the links in the chain for the class Preservation of bronze medals, using CC: notation: ND,72;5:98

Fine arts   N
   Sculpture   D
      Facet indicator for third level P facet   ,
        Numismatics   7
          Medals   2
           Facet indicator for M facet   ;
             Bronze   5
               Facet indicator for E facet   :
                 Others   9
                 Preservation   8

c) Chain procedure; False links; Hidden links; Hierarchy; Unsought links.

LINKS

a) Symbols which indicate the relative strength of the relationship between the various descriptors used to index a document in a term entry post-coordinate indexing system.

b) Links are an attempt to prevent false drops—to increase precision. Suppose a document on the effect of parental death on disturbed children were to be indexed under the descriptors Death; Parents; Children; and Emotional disturbance. This document would then be retrieved by enquirers looking for information on disturbed parents, or for the effect of children's death on parents, or for emotionally disturbed reactions to death—and it would be irrelevant for all of them. Now suppose that a common additional symbol were to be added to the document number posted on the cards headed Death and Parents—the illustration shows the letter A added to the document number 205 on Uniterm cards:

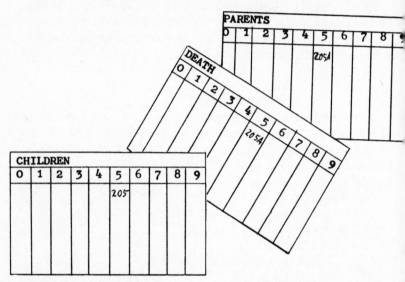

A trained user, pulling out the cards headed Parents and Emotional disturbance when looking for information on disturbed parents, will be warned off document number 205, because of the difference in the symbols—the links. (With optical coincidence cards, links take the form of differently-shaped holes).

The problem about links is that they warn off indiscriminately; for example, document number 205 is about a relationship between parents and children, but when these two cards are retrieved the links may cause the searcher to reject the document.

c) Partitioning; Roles

LITERAL MNEMONICS

a) Notational symbols which are memorable because they are letters which are the same as the initial letters of the name of the class in ordinary language; eg, in BC, U represents the class Useful arts, and within that class UA represents Agriculture.

c) Systematic mnemonics.

LITERARY UNIT

a) An independent work, which may be manifested in a number of different bibliographic units; eg, the work called *A sentimental journey* may be published in different editions at different times by different publishers; each edition will provide a different bibliographic unit to be catalogued. It might also appear bound with *Tristram Shandy,* or as part of *The collected works of Laurence Sterne,* or *The selected works of Laurence Sterne*; and each of these could result in a number of bibliographic units more.

c) Uniform title.

LITERARY WARRANT (1)

a) To include in a classification scheme a place for all classes which occur in the literature is to observe literary warrant. For example, if a work on spiders and insects were published, the class Spiders and insects should appear in the scheme, even though such a class would not appear in a zoological classification.

b) This principle was advanced by Wyndham Hulme in 1911. The development of faceted techniques has made it irrelevant.

c) Pigeon holes.

LITERARY WARRANT (2)

a) To base the construction of a classification scheme on an examination of the literature of the subject of the scheme, so that the classes and the structure of the scheme correspond to the needs of the documents which will be classified according to the scheme, and to the needs of users.

b) A particular instance of literary warrant is the decision whether or not to provide a specific class for a subject in DC, which is dependent on the volume of material available on that subject.

LOGICAL ADDITION *see* LOGICAL SUM

LOGICAL ANALYSIS *see* SEMANTIC FACTORS

LOGICAL DIFFERENCE

a) The logical operation in Boolean algebra which distinguishes one class from all others, producing the two classes X and not-X: the class whose members possess a quality, and the complementary class whose members do not possess that quality, shown in this diagram:

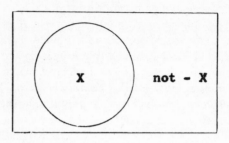

b) Logical difference is the basis for the search strategy involved in satisfying subject requests which include a negation, such as 'I want information on flintlock guns, but not information on military flintlocks'.

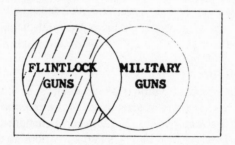

c) Boolean algebra; Conditional exclusion; Logical product; Logical sum; Optical coincidence cards; Venn diagrams.

LOGICAL DIVISION
   a) The process of deriving species from a genus.
   b) Since bibliographic classification schemes deal with other relationships, as well as the genus-species relationship, logical division is less important for indexing than it is for logical classification. In faceted classification schemes it is applied only within facets; in enumerative classification schemes it is more generally applied if

one allows an extended definition—the process of deriving sub-classes from a class.

The rules of logical division provide a vocabulary with which one can criticise classification schemes; these rules are: that one characteristic of division only should be applied to produce a step of division (otherwise cross-classification occurs); that steps of division should modulate—no step should be omitted (otherwise certain classes will be omitted, and some relationships not recognised); and that division should be exhaustive (otherwise, some classes will be omitted).

c) Boolean algebra; Mutually exclusive classes; Predicables; Syntagmatic relationships.

LOGICAL MULTIPLICATION *see* LOGICAL PRODUCT

LOGICAL OPERATIONS *see* BOOLEAN ALGEBRA

LOGICAL PRODUCT

a) The new class 'A *and* B', which is derived from the classes A and B by the logical operation of conjunction in Boolean algebra.

b) Superimposed classes and composite classes are examples of logical product, shown in such requests as 'I want information on how to catalogue maps', or 'I want information on military flint-locks'.

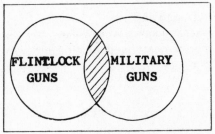

c) Logical difference; Logical sum; Venn diagrams.

LOGICAL SUBTRACTION *see* LOGICAL DIFFERENCE

LOGICAL SUM.

a) The new class 'A *or* B', derived from classes A and B by the logical operation of disjunction in Boolean algebra, and representing the joint membership of A and B.

b) Logical sum is the basis of the search strategy for enquiries such as 'What have you got on *either* hard drugs *or* hallucinogens'; 'I want books on *either* military guns *or* on flintlock guns'.

In information retrieval it is useful to assume that logical sum excludes logical product; eg, that the first enquirer in (b) does not want information on hallucinogenic hard drugs, and that the second does not want information on flintlock military guns.

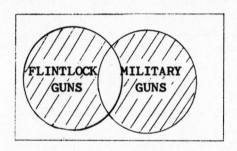

c) Logical difference; Venn diagrams.

LOOSE ASSEMBLAGES *see* COMPLEX CLASSES; PHASE RELATIONSHIPS

LOOSE LEAF CATALOGUES
a) Book form catalogues which allow the insertion of supplementary or replacement sheets, and the removal of sheets.
c) Sheaf catalogues.

M

MAIN CLASSES
a) In general classification schemes: discrete areas of knowledge which are coordinate with each other, and which together exhaust the universe.
b) Main classes are conventional divisions which vary from scheme to scheme; the number of such classes in a scheme seems

to depend largely on the notational base available—eg, DC has ten (using a numerical notation), while BC has twenty nine (using an alphabetical notation). The growth and decline of subjects, and the existence of inter-disciplinary subjects, cause problems in schemes based on main classes, and has led to a search for a more stable and rational basis for general classification schemes; of these, the use of integrative levels suggested for the proposed CRG scheme seems promising.

c) Basic classes; Canonical classes; Integrative levels; Partially comprehensive classes.

MAIN ENTRIES

a) The principal entry for a document in a catalogue giving the fullest information, is called the main entry.

b) The concept of main entry is important when there is a limitation on the number of entries which may be made for a document; if there is no limit dictated by cost, space or amount of work involved, entries could be made under all possible entry points without discrimination. Where there is a need to control the number of entries, to abbreviate the information given in some entries, or to record on one entry the tracings for a document, then a main entry must be chosen.

By convention, the main entry in a dictionary catalogue is the principal author entry; in a systematic catalogue it is the principal subject entry.

c) Added entries; Gradation by speciality; Order in array; Unit entries.

MANIPULATION INDEXES *see* POST-COORDINATE INDEXING SYSTEMS

MATTER

a) One of Ranganathan's fundamental categories; that to which facets representing materials are assigned; eg in Librarianship foci such as Printed books, Film strips and Patents appear in the Matter facet; in Sculpture, foci such as Wood, Marble, Bronze. Matter comes second in the citation order represented by PMEST.

MEET *see* LOGICAL PRODUCT

MEMORABILITY

a) The ease with which notation may be remembered, depending on its brevity, the kind of symbols used, its purity, and whether it has mnemonics.

MICROFORM CATALOGUES

a) These save space, and, when complete new catalogues are produced for a library at short intervals, are less expensive than paper copies and cause less volume of waste material.

c) Computer output microform.

MICROTHESAURI

a) Thesauri covering special fields which are absolutely compatible with a general thesaurus.

c) Satellite thesauri.

MIXED AUTHORSHIP

a) Composite authorship in which the contributions are of different kinds; eg, author/reviser; author/illustrator; nominal author/ghost.

c) Joint authorship.

MIXED NOTATION

a) Notation which uses more than one set of symbols; eg NarLpm (upper and lower case letters); 622.33(410) '17' (numerals and arbitrary symbols); NA52,C (upper case letters, numerals and arbitrary symbols).

b) Mixed notation has a longer base than pure notation, and provides facet indicators; but its use requires the searcher to learn the relative filing values of the different sets (eg, does Pinf file before or after PinGfn?).

MNEMONIC NOTATION

a) Notation whose meaning is easily memorised.

c) Literal mnemonics; Seminal mnemonics; Syllabic notation; Systematic mnemonics.

MODULATION

a) The avoidance of leaps in division, so that each step of division is proximate; that is, no step of division is omitted.

b) Consider this hierarchy:

Teaching aids

Books   Films   Filmstrips   Models   Slides   Realia

Because it breaks the rule of logical division that steps of division should modulate, or be proximate, it is not possible to specify certain classes—eg Audio-visual aids, Three-dimensional materials, Print material; and the relationship between certain classes is obscured—eg, that between Filmstrips and Slides, and that between Models and Realia.

A hierarchy which modulates looks like this:

Teaching aids

Print material   Audio-visual aids   Three-dimensional material

Books   Visual material   Models   Realia

Projected

Still   Moving

Slides   Filmstrips   Films

c) Bypassing references.

MONOGRAPH

a) A work conceived as a single entity; an independent work.

b) A monograph may be in more than one volume, and the volumes may be published successively, perhaps over many years. In some cases it may be difficult to distinguish such a work from a series, especially as earlier volumes may appear in new editions before later volumes make their first appearance. A suggested test is whether the publication programme is of finite length, which would indicate whether the author and publisher regarded the work as a single entity. By this test, some so-called series are revealed as multi-volume monographs; the extreme example is Pevsner's *Buildings of England*, called by the publisher *The buildings of England series*.

c) Serials.

MULTI-TOPICAL WORK *see* POLYTOPICAL WORK

MULTI-WORD SUBJECTS

a) A subject with more than one word in its name, so that an order between them must be decided in alphabetical subject headings.

c) Prepositional phrases; Significance order; Unit term.

MULTI-WORD TERMS *see* COMPOUND SUBJECTS (2); UNIT CONCEPTS

MULTIPLE AUTHORSHIP
a) A condition of authorship, in which more than one author is involved.

c) Composite work; Joint authorship; Mixed authorship; Principal authors; Subsidiary authors.

MULTIPLE ENTRY INDEXING SYSTEMS
a) Pre-coordinate indexing systems in which either more than one specific descriptor or entry term is made for a document, or a number of entries are made for the same document, one under a specific heading, the rest under general headings.

b) Multiple entry systems attempt to overcome the separations inevitable in single entry systems either by making multiple specific entry or by ensuring that each element in the descriptor or entry term is juxtaposed with each other element at some point in the index; or both. The increased ease of use is paid for by a larger index, and more work.

c) Combination indexing; Cycling; Permutation; Post-coordinate indexing systems; PRECIS; Rotation; Shunting; Single entry indexing systems; SLIC.

MUTUALLY EXCLUSIVE CLASSES
a) Classes which have no members in common; eg Birds/ Mammals; Gothic churches/Baroque churches; Smoothbore guns/ Rifled guns.

b) The principle that classes should be mutually exclusive is used in library classification when producing arrays of coordinate classes. The rule of logical division which results in mutually exclusive classes states that no more than one characteristic of division should be applied when producing steps of division. This hierarchy shows the result of failure to observe the rule:

	Pistols		
Breech loading	Muzzle loading	Rifled	Smoothbore

Because the two characteristics of 'How loaded' and 'Whether

92

rifled' have been applied together the classes in this array are not mutually exclusive—for example, it is possible to have a smooth-bore breech loading pistol—and cross-classification follows (should a work on smoothbore breech loading pistols be placed in the class smoothbore pistols or the class Breech loading pistols?) A hierarchy which obeys the rule avoids this difficulty:

Notice that it is only classes properly in array which are mutually exclusive—indeed, that it is not possible for other classes to be so. For example, the classes Testing and Pistols have the class Testing pistols in common; the classes Timber churches and Gothic churches have the class Timber gothic churches in common; and the classes Respiration and Birds have the class Respiration of birds in common. What class can Muzzle loading pistols and Breech loading pistols have in common?

N

NAME CATALOGUES

a) Interfiled author/title and subject catalogues, the subject entries being for subjects with proper names only; eg, works both by and about an author will be found in a name catalogue under his name.

b) If a name catalogue is used it is usually as a component of a systematic catalogue, but could be as part of a divided dictionary catalogue. The collocation of works by and about an author is useful, but causes filing problems; and the presence of some subject entries in an apparently author/title catalogue may be confusing, just as the absence of some entries from the subject component could be misleading.

c) Grouped headings.

NARROWER-BROADER ORDER

a) A filing order in which no works on broader subjects file before works on narrower subjects.

b) Assuming that the principle of inversion is observed, narrower-broader order will bring works on the primary facet to the front of the sequence, so giving prominence to what is thought to be the most important aspect of the subject; but broader-narrower order is more generally acceptable.

NATURAL CLASSIFICATION
a) Classification based solely on essential properties, displaying only the genus-species relationship.

b) As library classification must deal with other types of relationship as well as the genus-species relationship, natural classification is not a sufficient basis for it.

c) Artificial classification.

NATURAL LANGUAGE INDEXING SYSTEMS
a) Those whose index vocabularies are not controlled and structured at the time of indexing or of searching the index: keyword indexes.

b) Natural language systems are likely to have low recall, because synonyms and word-forms are not controlled, and because class inclusion relationships and other generic relationships are not revealed; but may have high precision, because if a match occurs between the term used by the enquirer and the descriptor it is likely to be a closer match than that between the enquirer's term and a synonym (there are very few absolute synonyms)—but this advantage is reduced, because of the failure to control homographs.

c) Articulated indexing systems; Controlled index vocabularies; Ordinary language indexing systems; Structured indexing systems.

NEGATION *see* LOGICAL DIFFERENCE

NEUTRAL INDEX
a) An alphabetical subject index constructed without reference to a particular classification scheme, and so equally usable with any.

c) Chain procedure; PRECIS.

NO CONFLICT
a) The cataloguing of new accessions according to new practice only if the result would not conflict with existing entries.

c) Attrition; Superimposition (2).

NOISE *see* FALSE DROPS

NON-SPECIFIC INDEXING

a) Indexing which uses descriptors of greater extension than the subjects of the documents being indexed.

b) Non-specific indexing is economical, and increases recall performance; it may be less daunting to inexperienced users than specificity; but except in small collections the loss of precision involved makes specificity preferable.

c) Broad classification; Close classification.

NORMALISED RECALL RATIO

a) The ratio $\dfrac{\text{sum of the recall ratio of all ranks}}{\text{number of ranks}}$ (where a rank is based on the ratio between the number of relevant and the number of non-relevant documents retrieved at different levels of search), used in measuring the recall performance of a system as a whole.

NOT RELATIONSHIP *see* LOGICAL DIFFERENCE

NOTATION

a) A code with an intelligible ordinal value which is attached to classes in a classification scheme to display and maintain the filing order of the scheme.

b) The code may be used as a means of easily shelving and finding documents shelved in systematic order; as the basis for order in the classified file; and for administrative purposes, eg for selective stock checking, issue counts etc.

c) Allocation; Arbitrary symbols; Arithmetical notation; Base; Brevity; Empty digits; Expressive notation; Facet indicators; Fence notation; Fractional notation; Gap notation; Group notation; Hierarchical notation; Hospitality; Memorability; Mixed notation; Mnemonic notation; Pure notation; Retroactive notation; Sector notation; Simplicity; Structural notation; Synthesis.

NOTES

a) Amplification of the standard description of a document, added by the cataloguer to further identify or characterise the document; eg, to elucidate an obscure title, to show the level of the work, to show its relationship to other works, to describe peculiarities in the copy being catalogued etc.

NOTHING BEFORE SOMETHING *see* WORD BY WORD

NOTIONAL ABSTRACTS
a) The sets of keywords which are extracted from a text because they occur with more than a certain frequency, translated mechanically into a standard form, and stored to form the data base of a mechanised indexing system.

NUMBER BUILDING *see* SYNTHESIS

O

OBJECTIVE INTENSION *see* INTENSION

OCTAVE NOTATION *see* SECTOR NOTATION

ON-LINE SYSTEMS
a) Computer systems which provide direct contact between the searcher and the machine during the searching operation.
c) Batch processing; Heuristic searches; Iterative searches.

ONE-APPROACH CATALOGUES
a) Catalogues which display records of required documents to an enquirer at his first entry into the catalogue; eg, a search under 'lions' reveals documents on this subject.
b) This advantage is claimed for the alphabetico-direct catalogue; it is lessened, however, by the possibility of choosing to search under the 'wrong' synonym, or the 'wrong' entry word in a multi-word subject.

ONE-FOCUS SIMPLE CLASSES *see* SIMPLE CLASSES

ONE HEADING PER ENTITY *see* UNIFORM HEADINGS

ONE PLACE CLASSIFICATION SCHEMES

a) Those which collocate documents on concretes (as does SC) may be claimed to be one-place schemes; but while all documents on, say, Coal may be found at one place, documents on other subjects—eg, economics, geology, mining—are inevitably scattered.

c) Aspect classification schemes; Citation order.

ONE PLACE INDEXING SYSTEMS *see* SINGLE ENTRY INDEXING SYSTEMS

OPEN ACCESS

a) Of a library which allows readers to select documents direct from the shelves.

b) Open access allows readers freedom, and enables them to browse among documents and broaden, narrow and extend searches on the shelves rather than among document surrogates. It requires a helpful shelf order.

c) Closed access.

OPEN ENTRY

a) Catalogue entry with incomplete description, because the work is in progress or the library is for some other reason waiting to complete its set; or because the work is a serial.

OPTICAL COINCIDENCE CARDS

a) Term entry cards on which document numbers are posted as holes in standard positions; holes common to more than one card are revealed by holding the squared-up set against a light source.

b) This form of term entry avoids the tedious and inefficient scanning associated with Uniterm cards. Refinements in the form of coloured transparent sheets to lay between cards to express relationships of exclusion ('I want documents on firearms, but not on military firearms') and conditional exclusions ('I want documents on firearms, but not on military firearms unless they're handguns') are available.

OR RELATIONSHIP *see* LOGICAL SUM

ORDER IN ARRAY

a) The filing order of coordinate classes, such as main classes, canonical classes in CC, and foci in a facet.

b) Helpful orders in array—other than alphabetical order—include canonical order; chronological order; increasing complexity; size; spatial proximity.

c) Favoured category; Gradation by speciality.

ORDINAL NOTATION

a) Non-hierarchical notation: notation which merely shows the order of classes, without displaying their superordinate-subordinate-coordinate relationships by its length; eg, from LECI:

Tab	Exceptional children
Tap	Handicapped
Tas	Physically handicapped
Teb	Blind
Tef	Deaf
Tib	Mentally handicapped
Tik	Retarded

b) Ordinal notation produces brevity, and does not interfere with hospitality.

ORDINARY LANGUAGE INDEXING SYSTEMS

a) Systems whose vocabulary is controlled and structured, and consists of the names of concepts in ordinary language; eg, alphabetico-direct catalogue headings.

c) Alphabetico-classed catalogues; Natural language indexing systems; Subject heading lists; Systematic catalogues; Thesauri.

P

PMEST

a) The facet formula for the citation order of the fundamental categories Personality, Matter, Energy, Space, Time in CC.

c) Levels; Rounds.

PAGINATION

a) The statement of the number of pages in the description of a document, indicating the extent of the work. It is usual to include a statement of the number of plates in the pagination statement.

PAIRED KEYWORD INDEXING

a) Indexing in which each pair of terms in the subject statement are juxtaposed to provide descriptors; eg, for a document entitled *Play therapy for the maladjusted child*:

Child
   maladjusted
Child
   play therapy
Maladjusted
   child
Maladjusted
   play therapy
Play therapy
   child
Play therapy
   maladjusted

b) An example is provided by the Permuterm index in *Science citation index* and *Social science citation index*.

c) Double-KWIC; Permutation.

PARADIGM

a) The set of varied forms of a word produced by conjugation or declension; so, by extension, the set of words which have the same root; eg, catalog, catalogue, catalogues, cataloguing, cataloging, recataloguing.

b) The control of word forms increases the recall performance of an indexing system, but may decrease precision.

c) Confounding; Truncation.

PARADIGMATIC RELATIONSHIP *see* GENUS-SPECIES RELATIONSHIP; SYNTAGMATIC RELATIONSHIPS

PARALLEL SEQUENCES

a) A number of sequences of items, the order within each sequence being the same.

b) The most obvious example, and the one which causes difficulty in most libraries, is the various sequences of documents on shelves—lending sequence, reference sequence, oversize sequence etc. The separation of related material caused by parallel sequences should be overcome in the catalogue.

c) Broken order; Sequence symbols.

PARTIALLY COMPREHENSIVE CLASSES
a) Main classes which are superordinate to other main classes; the term is Ranganathan's, and CC provides examples such as Natural sciences, which includes the main classes Physics, Engineering, Chemistry, Zoology etc; Humanities, which includes the main classes Fine arts, Literature, Religion and Philosophy; and Social sciences, which includes Education, Economics and Law. Some of CC's partially comprehensive classes have Greek letters as notation; eg $\leq$ (sigma) for Social sciences.

PARTITIONING
a) A device to increase precision in post-coordinate indexing systems in which depth indexing is practised. Suppose a document on naval swords is indexed in depth, and two of the subthemes are Decoration of dress swords and Blade shapes of fighting swords. The descriptors will be 1) Blade shapes; 2) Decoration; 3) Dress swords; 4) Fighting swords. As a result, false drops may occur; eg, this document will be retrieved by an enquirer looking for information on the decoration of fighting swords. Partitioning avoids this, by treating each subtheme as though it were a separate document; in item entry systems, a separate card can be made for each subtheme, and in term entry systems a different number can be assigned to each subtheme (although each number will lead to the same document description in the associated document index, of course).
c) Links.

PASTED SLIP CATALOGUES *see* GUARDBOOK CATALOGUES

PEEK-A-BOO CARDS *see* OPTICAL COINCIDENCE CARDS

PEEPHOLE CARDS *see* OPTICAL COINCIDENCE CARDS

PERMUTATION INDEXING
a) A multiple entry indexing system which produces a specific statement at every entry point, and juxtaposes each element with each other element; eg
Cataloguing. Maps. University libraries

Cataloguing. University libraries. Maps
Maps. Cataloguing. University libraries
Maps. University libraries. Cataloguing
University libraries. Cataloguing. Maps
University libraries. Maps. Cataloguing.
In addition, references from synonyms and from the names of re-
lated classes are necessary.

b) Permutation may be used in alphabetical subject catalogues,
in classified catalogues provided that the notation is expressive,
and in alphabetical subject indexes; but it is very uneconomic, and
cannot be recommended. The number of entries generated is given
by N! (factorial N), where N = the number of elements; for example,
with 3 elements, $3 \times 2 \times 1$ entries are generated; with 4 elements,
$4 \times 3 \times 2 \times 1$; with 5, $5 \times 4 \times 3 \times 2 \times 1$.

c) Combination indexing; Cycling; Paired keyword index; Rotation; Shunting; SLIC

PERMUTERM INDEX

a) Name given to the paired keyword indexes in *Science citation index* and *Social science citation index*.

b) This is not, as its name might indicate, a true permuted index,
because it is not intended to produce specific descriptors; its effect
is more like that of Double-KWIC.

PERSONAL AUTHORSHIP

a) Authorship by individuals as opposed to authorship by
groups of people acting as corporate bodies. Personal authorship
does not imply that only one author is involved.

PERSONALITY

a) One of Ranganathan's fundamental categories, the primary
facet in the facet formula PMEST, to which foci peculiar to the class
or representing the purpose of the class are assigned; eg, in Zoology, kinds of animals; in Librarianship, kinds of libraries; in Psychology, kinds of people.

PERVASIVE SUBJECTS

a) Subjects included in Generalia classes because they are
thought to be useful in all, or a great many, of the subject classes;
eg Education, Logic.

101

PHASE RELATIONSHIPS

a) Relationships in which the elements remain distinct, and do not lose their identities in the new class produced by the relationship. The new classes produced by phase relationships are called complex classes (Ranganathan also calls them 'loose assemblages').

b) Examples of phase relationships are shown below:

A comparison between steam locomotives and diesel locomotives.

The influence of Horace Walpole on the gothic revival.

The relationship between physical traits and intellectual ability.

These show that phase relationships cannot be predicted, but must be dealt with as they arise in particular documents. This is a notational problem.

c) Bias phase relationship; Comparison phase relationship; Composite classes; Compound classes; Exposition phase; Influence phase relationship.

PHASES

a) The elements which compose a complex class.

c) Phase relationships.

PHYSICAL FORMS OF CATALOGUE

a) As opposed to the file organisation of the catalogue; any one file organisation may be presented in any of a number of physical forms.

b) The criteria for choice of a physical form are its ease of use—whether it permits easy scanning of a number of entries, whether it is portable, whether one user prevents many others from using it, whether it is easily guided, whether insertion and removal of entries is easy; and its cost, in terms of capital expenditure, continuing cost of materials, cost of staff time and space taken.

c) Accessibility; Book form catalogues; Card catalogues; Computer output microform; Flexibility (2); Guardbook catalogues; Loose leaf catalogues; Microform catalogues; Post-coordinate indexing system; Portability; Sheaf catalogues; Strip indexes; Visible indexes.

PHYSICAL FORMS OF DOCUMENT

a) The form of the physical carrier of the message—printed

book, film loop, periodical, gramophone record etc—as opposed to the form of presentation of the message.

b) Distinguish between a physical form and a work about a physical form; between a filmstrip and a work about filmstrips (because LEC2 lacks a common form facet, students and other users may be tempted to use the subject class Filmstrip when expressing a physical form of document—eg, when constructing notation for a filmstrip on road safety; the temptation should be resisted). Notice the ambiguity inherent in certain forms; for example, a map is both a form of presentation and—usually—a physical form of document. The form of presentation is a problem for the indexer; the physical form is really a management problem—how to store the document.

PLATES

a) A kind of page: pages which bear illustrations, and which are not counted in the pagination of the text pages.

POLYTOPICAL WORK

a) A work on more than one distinct subject, in which there is no interaction between the subjects: in effect, more than one work bound between the same pair of covers or issued in the same document; eg *Naval and military swords; How to look after rabbits, gerbils and hamsters.*

b) If the subjects covered exhaust, or nearly exhaust, a superordinate class the work should be treated as though it were on that class; eg, a work entitled *The clarinet, basset horn and saxophone* should be indexed as a work on single-reed woodwind instruments; otherwise, each subject should be separately indexed, as far as an agreed economic limit.

c) Composite classes; Superimposed classes.

POST-COORDINATE INDEXING SYSTEMS

a) Systems whose descriptors are in the form of isolates, so that a document whose subject has more than one element must be given a separate descriptor for each element; eg, in a term entry post-coordinate system a document entitled *Teaching French by the direct method in primary schools* would be entered on three cards whose headings would be, respectively, French language; Primary schools; and Direct teaching method. At the search stage, documents entered under each of the search terms are compared to discover which are common to all terms; this process may be facilitated by the use of optical or mechanical devices.

b) Post-coordinate systems increase the recall performance for any isolate; are easier to compile than pre-coordinate indexing systems because the indexer does not need to construct specific descriptors involving choice of citation order, with guides from alternative approaches; and may reduce clerical work. On the other hand, the size of file is limited; for practical reasons these systems cannot be used by untrained enquirers; the number of enquirers who can use a postcoordinate index at one time is very limited; and, above all, precision suffers, so that post-coordinate systems are likely to yield a high number of false drops.

c) Coding; Item entry systems; Links; Partitioning; Posting; Roles; Weighting.

POSTING

a) The entry of document numbers on Uniterm or optical coincidence cards.

c) Coding; Terminal digit posting.

PRECATALOGUING

a) Cataloguing a work before publication, to decrease the time lag between publication of a work and its appearance in the catalogue.

b) Precataloguing depends on the cooperation of publishers, in making proofs available, or in advertising their forthcoming publications in some detail; and there is the possibility of changes in the document between cataloguing and publication. BNB's proposed precataloguing has been called by them cataloguing in publication; this seems an unhelpful name, as that term has an already accepted meaning.

c) Centralised cataloguing.

PRECIS

a) PREserved Context Indexing System: a multiple specific entry indexing system developed to replace chain indexing in BNB. The order of elements is based on the principle of context dependency, shown by relational operators, which preserves the meaning in every entry. After the intellectual part of the indexing process has been completed by human indexers (that is, up to the formation of the concept string of elements in order) the elements are shunted by computer to bring each significant element to the filing position, using a two-line format; eg:

Secondary schools
    Curriculum. Geography. Field work   RefNibLax
Curriculum. Secondary schools
    Geography. Field work   RefNibLax
Geography. Curriculum. Secondary schools
    Field work   RefNibLax
Field work. Geography. Curriculum. Secondary schools RefNibLax.

In addition, references from synonyms and from related classes are made; eg Syllabus *see* Curriculum; Schools *see also* Secondary schools; Earth sciences *see also* Geography.

b) Unlike chain procedure, PRECIS is not dependent on any classification scheme; is easily computerised; and provides multiple specific entries. As a technique for subject analysis it has possibilities outside its use in BNB.

c) Cycling; Display; Lead; Qualifier; Rotation; Shunting.

PRECISION

a) A measure of the efficiency of an indexing system, shown by the ratio $\dfrac{\text{number of relevant documents retrieved}}{\text{total number of documents retrieved}} \times \dfrac{100}{1}$.

b) The precision performance of an indexing system tends to vary inversely with its recall performance.

c) Close classification; Controlled index vocabularies; Links; Partitioning; Qualifiers; Ranking; Roles.

PRE-COORDINATE INDEXING SYSTEMS

a) Indexing systems in which the descriptor is also a specifier; that is, in which descriptors are as specific statements of the subjects of documents as the system allows. The two usual examples of pre-coordinate systems are classified catalogues and alphabetico-direct catalogues.

b) Pre-coordination involves a choice of citation order for elements, with a consequent scattering of some related documents unless a form of absolute multiple entry is used.

c) Post-coordinate indexing systems; Single entry entry indexing systems.

PREDICABLES

a) The concepts used in distinguishing the species of a genus.

b) Aristotle recognised five predicables: genus, definition, difference, property and accident; Porphyry replaced definition by species, to give the current five predicables.

c) Logical division; Predicates.

PREDICATES

a) Statements made about subjects, especially when made in an attempt to define them; eg 'Man is a thinking animal'.

c) Predicables; Properties.

PREFERRED CATEGORY *see* FAVOURED CATEGORY

PREFERRED ORDER *see* CITATION ORDER; SIGNIFICANCE ORDER

PRENATAL CATALOGUING *see* CATALOGUING IN PUBLICATION; PRECATALOGUING

PREPOSITIONAL PHRASES

a) The prepositional phrase form is the preferred ordinary language form used by Coates as the basis for significance order in multi-word subject headings; before deciding on significance order, multi-word subjects whose names do not include prepositions are amplified to form prepositional phrases—Child psychology is changed to Psychology of children, for example. The result decides the order of elements in the heading; eg.

amplified phrase	*heading*
cataloguing of maps	Maps—Cataloguing
partitions of buildings	Buildings—Partitions
toxicity of paint	Paint—Toxicity
(but: Canoes of canvas	Canoes—Canvas)

Other prepositions reveal relationships on which order is based in a similar way:

engines operated by steam	Steam engines
firearms with flintlocks	Firearms—Flintlocks

c) Alphabetico-direct subject catalogues; Significance order.

PRESERVED CONTEXT INDEXING SYSTEM *see* PRECIS

PREPUBLICATION CATALOGUING *see* PRECATALOGUING

PRIMARY AUTHORS

a) Those who create a work, as opposed to those who contribute to a bibliographic unit which depends on the work—eg, editors, illustrators, translators, compilers of anthologies etc.

c) Principal authors; Secondary authors.

PRIMARY FACETS

a) Those which are cited first, so that their documents are collocated by the citation order.

c) Distributed relatives; Personality.

PRINCIPAL AUTHORS

a) In works of multiple authorship, those to whom principal responsibility is attributed.

c) Primary authors; Subsidiary authors.

PRODUCT *see* PURPOSE

PROFILE

a) A record of a client's interests, against which accessions may be matched, or an existing store searched, to discover relevant documents.

c) Search strategy; Selective dissemination of information.

PRONOUNCEABLE NOTATION *see* SYLLABIC NOTATION

PROPERTY

a) One of the five predicables: an attribute possessed by all members of a species which is nevertheless not essential to its definition; eg, all firearms have barrels, but possession of a barrel is not part of the definition of a firearm.

c) Accident; Difference.

PROXIMATE STEPS OF DIVISION *see* MODULATION

PSEUDONYMOUS AUTHORSHIP
a) Authorship indicated by an assumed name which is sufficient as an identification.

c) Anonymous authorship.

PUNCH ALSO
a) The instruction in a thesaurus to make a generic entry for a document, as well as a specific entry; eg Mexico *punch also* Central America.

PUNCHED CARDS
a) Item entry cards with numbered positions on the face, each position or combination of positions representing a concept. A document's isolates are coded as holes at the appropriate positions. Punched card files are searched with mechanical or electrical machines, and require trained operators.

c) Edge notched cards; Item term cards.

PURE NOTATION
· a) Notation consisting solely of one set of symbols: A–Z, or a–z, or 0–9.

b) The filing order of pure notation is obvious and easy to use; but its base is shorter than that of mixed notation, and a pure notation cannot have facet indicators, so that a faceted scheme with pure notation must use it in retroactive form.

PURPOSE
a) A guide in choosing citation order: the facet which reflects the purpose or end product of the subject should be cited before all others; eg, in Agriculture, Crops should be cited before Operations; in Librarianship, Libraries before Materials or Operations; in Education, Students before Curriculum or Teaching method.

PYRAMID CODING
a) A fixed field indirect coding system for edge notched cards, which allows any number from 0–9 to be encoded in each field of five holes, without false drops. The encoded number is shown by opening the two holes which are its coordinates; eg, number 4 is

encoded here:

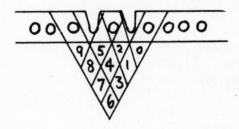

Q

QUALIFIER
   a) The terms which follow the entry word on the first line of a
PRECIS entry; eg, 'university libraries' in
Maps. University libraries
   Cataloguing.
   c) Display; Lead.

QUALIFIERS
   a) Terms added to entry words to control homographs or to
show the context of the entry word; eg
   Bridges (Civil engineering)
   Bridges (Electrical engineering)
and
   Children: Care 649.1
   Children: Medicine 618.92
   Children: Psychology 159.922.7
   Children: Social welfare 362.7.
   c) Chain procedure; Relative index; Roles; Scope notes; Sub-
headings.

QUASI-ISOLATES
   a) Characteristics of division listed in the schedules of a classification scheme as though they were classes, to guide the classifier;
eg

Persons	D
(by class)	
Working class	D1
Middle class	D2
Upper class	D3
(by age)	
Young people	D4
Children	D5
Adolescents	D6
Adults	D7
Young	D8
Middle aged	D9
Old	D10
(by sex)	
Female	D11
Male	D12

b) The name seems to come from the fact that these quasi-isolates could also be actual classes in other facets; for example, 'sex' and 'class' could be classes in their own right.

c) Subfacets.

R

RADIX FRACTIONS *see* FRACTIONAL NOTATION

RANDOM ACCESS *see* DIRECT ACCESS

RANDOM CODING *see* SUPERIMPOSED RANDOM CODING

RANKING

a) Placing documents in an order which reflects the degree to which they match the search terms.

b) Ranking enables the most relevant documents to be selected, and in mechanised systems enables a cut-off point to be used, which results in the suppression of documents whose rank is below a predetermined level.

c) Ranges.

REAL TIME *see* ON LINE SYSTEMS

RECALL

a) A measure of the efficiency of an indexing system; the ratio

$$\frac{\text{number of relevant documents retrieved}}{\text{number of relevant documents in collection}} \times \frac{100}{1}$$

b) The recall performance of an indexing system tends to vary inversely with its precision performance.

c) Broad classification; Close classification; Controlled index vocabularies; Generic entry; Normalised recall ratio; Specificity; Structured index vocabularies.

RECIPROCAL ENTRIES

a) Instructions in a thesaurus or other indexing tool which complement each other; as

Adolescents	Teenagers
Use for Teenagers	*Use* Adolescents

REFERENCES

a) Instructions which lead the catalogue user from one heading to another.

b) References are usually made to the heading chosen for the document being catalogued. *See* references lead from an unused heading to the preferred heading; eg, from one of an author's names to the uniform heading, as in

Corvo, *Baron see* Rolfe, Frederick

or from an entry word to a descriptor:

Wireless *see* Radio

See also references lead from a related heading which may be used for some works to the heading chosen for the work being catalogued; eg

Dodgson, Charles Lutwidge *see also* Carroll, Lewis

Mathematics *see also* Arithmetic.

c) Bypassing references; Downward references; Reciprocal entries; Syndetic structure; Upward references.

RELATED WORKS

a) Independent works which owe their existence to some earlier work are related to that work, and vice-versa; examples include sequels and replies.

c) Dependent works.

RELATIONAL INDEXING

a) Techniques which concentrate on the expression of the precise relationship between concepts, using relational operators; eg PRECIS and Farradane's relational indexing.

c) Analets.

RELATIONAL OPERATORS

a) Symbols which represent a relationship between concepts, such as those used to determine the order in a PRECIS concept string; eg

Oxfordshire (0) Schools (1) Students (p) Transport (2) Buses (3) in which (0) = Environment (the schools are IN Oxfordshire)

         (1) = Key system (the work is about schools)

         (p) = Part (students are a PART of the school)

         (2) = Action (something that happens to the students)

         (3) = Agent (of the action—they're transported BY bus)

c) Analets; Relational indexing.

RELATIVE INDEXES

a) Indexes to a classified file or to a classification scheme which display relationships; especially those relationships which are obscured by the scheme's citation order; eg:

Children: Care   649.1

Children: Medicine   618.92

Children: Psychology   159.922.7

Children: Social welfare   362.7

Documents on the subject Children are badly scattered by this classification scheme, as the notations show; but at least all notations relevant to the subject are gathered together under the name of the subject in the relative index.

b) The relative index was one of Melvil Dewey's contributions to indexing; in his introduction to DC12, published in 1927, he calls the 'Relative Subject Index' 'the most important feature of the sistem'.

c) Chain procedure; Distributed relatives; Specific indexes.

RELATIVE LOCATION

a) The system of locating documents by their positions relative to each other, usually according to classification notation or author's name.

b) Relative location allows for the insertion of new documents in the sequence, and so is necessary if a helpful shelf order—such as systematic order—is required, as in open access libraries.

c) Fixed location; Sequential location.

RELEVANCE see PRECISION

REPEATER DIGITS see FENCE NOTATION; SECTOR NOTATION

REPRINT

a) A new impression of a printed book, with no substantial changes.

c) Edition; Facsimile reprint; Issue.

RETROACTIVE NOTATION

a) A form of expressive notation which does not rely upon facet indicators, and so is able to retain purity. The facets are filed in the reverse of citation order, and this order is maintained by an introductory digit. Within each facet, no digit of lesser filing value than the introductory digit may be used; eg

D	Library operations
DD	Acquisition
DE	Indexing
DF	Circulation
E	Library materials
EE	Printed materials
EEE	Books
EEF	Serials
EF	Non-print materials
EFE	Audio-visual material
EFF	Sound recordings
F	Libraries
FF	Public
FG	Academic
FH	Special

As a result, a synthetic notation has its structure displayed by drops in filing value of digits; eg, the notation for the class Indexing sound recordings in academic libraries is FGEFFDE, which is clearly made up from FG EFF DE.

b) Retroactive notation fulfills the three functions of expressiveness, while avoiding the difficulties of mixed notation; but the citation order chosen by the maker of the scheme cannot be changed, and the notational base becomes increasingly shorter as the facets near the primary facet; which is why letter notations are preferred for this form of notation.

c) Fence notation.

ROLE OPERATORS *see* RELATIONAL OPERATORS

ROLES

a) Qualifiers which define the function of a descriptor, usually in a post-coordinate indexing system; eg

Librarians (Agents)

Librarians (Patients)

The first descriptor would be used for documents with titles such as *The librarian as educator*; the second for documents such as *The education of the librarian*.

b) Roles increase precision by narrowing the descriptors, and also by indicating the direction of a relationship; eg, the ambiguity produced by indexing the work *The effect of parental suicide on children* under Children; Parents; Suicide could be reduced by adding a role to Children indicating that term's passive situation—giving Children (patients); Parents; Suicide.

c) Links; Scope notes.

ROOF LANGUAGE *see* INTERMEDIATE LEXICON

ROOT WORD *see* PARADIGM; TRUNCATION

ROTATION

a) A multiple specific entry indexing system, in which each element in turn is brought to the filing position but the relative order of elements is unchanged; eg

Decoration. Flintlock. Hunting. Rifles

Rifles. Decoration. Flintlock. Hunting

Hunting. Rifles. Decoration. Flintlock

Flintlock. Hunting. Rifles. Decoration

In addition, references from synonyms and from the names of related classes would need to be made; eg Snaphaunce *see also* Flintlock; Sporting *see also* Hunting.

b) Rotation produces as many entries as there are elements; each entry is specific, but elements are not juxtaposed; for example, an enquirer looking for documents on Flintlock rifles would not discover the work indexed in (a) easily.

Rotation may be used in alphabetical catalogues; in classified catalogues, provided that the notation is fully expressive; and in alphabetical subject indexes.

c) Combination indexing; Cycling; KWIC; Permutation indexing; PRECIS; Shunting.

ROUNDS

a) The fundamental categories of CC may be manifested more than once; for example, an Energy facet may have its own Personality facet (kinds of the actions or properties) or its own Energy facet (actions on actions or properties; eg Prevention of crime). These different manifestations of the same category are called rounds.

b) The primary manifestation is called the first round; thus, First Round Personality (symbol: [P]), First Round Energy (symbol: [E]). Later manifestations are second or third rounds; eg Third Round Personality—[3P]—and Second Round Energy—[2E].

An example of a facet formula including rounds is Y [P] : [E] [2P] ; [2E] [3P], in which Y is the notation for the main class Sociology; [P] is the First Round Personality facet, with foci such as Children, Indians; [E] is the First Round Energy facet, together with its own Second Round Personality facet, containing foci such as Crime, Ceremonial (ie kinds of action); [2E] is the Second Round Energy facet with its own Third Round Personality facet, containing foci such as Influence, Prevention (actions on the actions in the First Round Energy facet).

c) Levels.

RULES OF LOGICAL DIVISION *see* LOGICAL DIVISION

S

SBN *see* INTERNATIONAL STANDARD BOOK NUMBER

SDI *see* SELECTIVE DISSEMINATION OF INFORMATION

SATELLITE THESAURI
a) Thesauri developed for special fields on the basis of a general thesaurus.
c) Microthesauri.

SCHEDULE ORDER
a) The order in which classes are arranged on the pages of a classification scheme.
b) Schedule order is not necessarily the same as filing order; the schedule order of CC is the same as citation order, but the correct filing order—the reverse of citation order—is produced by the facet indicators.
c) Inversion; Order in array; Shelf order.

SCHEDULES
a) The classes arranged on the pages of a classification scheme.
c) Alphabetical subject index; Notation.

SCOPE NOTES
a) Indications of the meaning or extension of terms in a thesaurus or subject headings list, or of a class in a classification scheme; eg
Film   Pay
SN Study of, as part of curriculum
Film   Lop
SN As teaching aid
(from LEC2 thesaurus)
027.4 Public libraries
Institutions that serve free all the residents of a community, district or region, usually receiving their financial support, in whole or in part, from public funds.
(from DC 17).

c) Qualifiers; Roles; Subheadings.

SEARCH LOGIC *see* BOOLEAN ALGEBRA; SEARCH STRATEGY

SEARCH PROFILE *see* PROFILE

SEARCH STRATEGY
a) The plan of a search for information, involving specification of needs, choice of search terms, degree of specificity in searching, how to extend the search to broader, narrower and related classes.

c) Boolean algebra; Browsing; Guiding; Heuristic searches; Iterative searches; Serendipity.

SEARCH THESAURUS
a) A thesaurus which displays to the enquirer relationships between natural language terms, to remind him of possibly useful entry terms in a natural language indexing system.

SECONDARY AUTHORS
a) Those whose contribution to a bibliographic unit depends on the previous work of a primary author; eg illustrators, translators, adaptors.

b) The statement of secondary authorship in the description of books must be related to the edition statement; notice the difference between

1) A classification of canoeing, by D W Hope; illustrated by F Smith 2nd ed.

and

2) A classification of canoeing, by D W Hope. 2nd ed, illustrated by F Smith.

c) Subsidiary authors.

SECTOR NOTATION
a) An attempt to combine hospitality and a hierarchical notation, in CC. The final digit of the base is reserved as a 'repeater', and is not considered to contribute to the length of the notation; by this fiction the notation 996 (lightning protection, in the main class Engineering) may be said to look coordinate with 95 (lighting, with which it is in this class coordinate).

c) Group notation.

SEGMENTATION

a) A device to indicate where a notation may meaningfully be shortened for local needs; used in BNB—eg 519.5'02'4309.

b) The author once worked in a library in which a junior assistant was given the job of shortening BNB's class numbers (before segmentation was introduced) by lopping off any digits beyond the third from the decimal point; this unintelligent procedure resulted in notations such as 616.100 and 940.540!

SELECTIVE CATALOGUING

a) Limited cataloguing applied to certain classes of documents; eg, no author entries for modern maps; author/title entries only for literary texts; no imprint or collation for modern books etc.

SELECTIVE DISSEMINATION OF INFORMATION

a) An individualised notification service, usually computerised, by which clients are informed of the receipt of new accessions which match their profile.

SELECTIVE LISTING IN COMBINATION see SLIC

SELF-CATALOGUING see CATALOGUING IN PUBLICATION

SEMANTIC ANALYSIS see SEMANTIC FACTORS

SEMANTIC CODE

a) The code used to represent WRU's telegraphic abstracts, based upon semantic factors. Each semantic factor is given a four-letter code, made up of a three-letter stem representing a broad concept and an additional letter (the semantic infix) to narrow the concept; eg D-CM = Information; DWCM = Brings about information. A complete code for a concept would look like this: DWCM.LQCT.MACH.TURN.001, in which DWCM = bringing about information; LQCT = using electricity; MACH = is a device; TURN = produces transmission; and 001 is an individualising suffix for a particular instrument which transmits information by electricity—the telephone. (The example is taken from Lancaster's *Vocabulary control*).

SEMANTIC FACTORS

a) Descriptors used in place of a common term which they define; eg, the descriptors Male and Parents, used in a post-coordinate system to index a work on Fathers; Device, Measurement, Heat used to index a work on Thermometers (see under Semantic code for another example).

b) Developed at WRU as a means of specifying any concept by the synthesis of general concepts. The practical advantages are increased recall performance for the semantic factors, and a smaller index vocabulary; the disadvantages, more work for the indexers and searchers, and more false drops (WRU experimented with links and roles in an attempt to overcome this).

c) Telescoping; Unit concepts.

SEMANTIC INFIX *see* SEMANTIC CODE

SEMINAL MNEMONICS

a) Notational symbols for general concepts (such as 'abnormality', 'structure' 'energy') which enable the indexer to expand an area of a classification scheme while waiting for a new edition to be produced, knowing that the notation he has used is likely to be that used in the new edition.

c) Hospitality.

SEPARATORS *see* FENCE NOTATION

SEQUENCE SYMBOLS

a) Symbols which indicate in which sequence a document is placed; eg R = reference library; O = Oversize.

SEQUENTIAL ACCESS

a) A search technique in a computer store which involves an examination of every record to discover the required information.

c) Direct access.

SEQUENTIAL LOCATION

a) The system of locating documents relative to each other, but without allowing insertions within the sequence; for example, by the use of accession numbers.

b) Sequential location saves space—there is no need to leave room for insertions at the ends of shelves; shelving is easier, and if necessary whole blocks of documents may be moved without changing location symbols; but helpful order is not possible, because insertions within the sequence cannot be made, so that this form of location should be confined to closed access libraries.

c) Fixed location; Relative location.

SEQUENTIAL SCANNING

a) Searching through a whole sequence of items to discover those required.

b) This may be necessary because of failure to collocate adequately, or merely because the enquirer wishes to browse.

c) Physical forms of catalogue; Serendiptiy.

SERENDIPITY

a) 'This discovery, indeed, is almost of that kind I call Serendipity, a very expressive word . . . you will understand it better by the derivation than by the definition. I once read a very silly fairy tale called *The three princes of Serendip* [Serendip = Sri Lanka]; as their highnesses travelled, they were always making discoveries, by accidents and sagacity, of things which they were not in quest of . . .'—Horace Walpole: Letter to Sir Horace Mann, 28th January 1754.

c) Browsing.

SERIALS

a) Part-works of indefinite extent, such as periodicals.

c) Monographs; Series.

SERIES

a) A set of independent works, each of which is related by common subject matter, approach, or presentation, issued by a publisher under a common series title or in a common format, or both; eg, New naturalist series; Oxford standard authors.

b) To be distinguished from serials, multi-volume monographs and parts of a publisher's output which happen to be given a name (eg Pelican books).

A series statement may be an important element in the characterisation of a work.

SHARED AUTHORSHIP *see* MULTIPLE AUTHORSHIP

SHARED CATALOGUING *see* COOPERATIVE CATALOGUING

SHEAF CATALOGUES
a) A physical form of catalogue with one entry on each slip; the slips, of typing paper thickness, are locked into binders.

b) Sheaf catalogues are portable, convenient to handle, easy to reproduce in multiple copies (using carbon paper); but are less flexible than card catalogues, not easy to scan, and subject to damage at the edges of slips.

c) Loose leaf catalogues.

SHELF LIST
a) A list of documents in the order in which they appear on the shelves.

SHELF MARKS
a) Symbols which show the document's filing position: call numbers.

c) Shelf notation.

SHELF NOTATION
a) Notation used to locate documents on shelves, as opposed to that used to arrange records of the documents in catalogues.

b) Shelf notation may be an abbreviated form of the notation used in the classified file, to make shelving and searching easier, while providing specificity in the catalogue. An exotic service would be provided by the use of one classification scheme for the order in the classified file and a different scheme for shelf order, so that entirely different collocations would occur.

c) Call number.

SHELF ORDER
a) The order of documents on shelves.

c) Filing order; Linear sequence; Schedule order.

SHUNTING
a) Austin's name for the rotation practised in BNB's PRECIS:

1) University libraries
   Maps, Cataloguing
2) Maps. University libraries
   Cataloguing
3) Cataloguing. Maps. University libraries.
   c) Cycling; Display; Lead; Qualifier.

SIBLING REFERENCES *see* HORIZONTAL REFERENCES

SIGNIFICANCE ORDER

a) An order for elements in an alphabetical subject heading based on the degree to which each element 'evokes the clearest mental image' (Coates) and is therefore memorable; the order is from more significant to less significant; eg Pipes. Concrete. Tests.

b) Coates derived this principle from an examination of Kaiser's Concrete-Process order, and developed it as the basis for his theory of order in alphabetical subject headings exemplified in BTI.

c) Citation order; Standard citation order.

SIMPLE CLASSES

a) Classes which represent one kind of thing in the context of a basic class. The kind of thing may be defined by more than one characteristic; eg, each of the following is a simple class: Direct teaching method; Firearms; Owls; Middle class, middle aged, maladjusted males.

b) In a faceted classification scheme, simple classes are either single foci or are expressed by the synthesis of notation from different subfacets in the same facet—that is, by superimposition; the latter are called superimposed classes. Perhaps one should call the former one-focus simple classes; or simple simple classes.

c) Composite classes.

SIMPLICITY

a) A quality of notation: the ease with which it conveys to the user the location of documents; it depends on brevity, the kind of symbols used (especially whether the notation is mixed or pure, and whether arbitrary symbols are present) and on the presence of devices which break the notation into intelligible sections.

c) Memorability.

SIMPLIFIED CATALOGUING *see* LIMITED CATALOGUING

SINGLE ENTRY INDEXING SYSTEMS

a) Pre-coordinate indexing systems in which documents receive only one entry, and only one entry term is specific; eg, the conventional classified file with a relative index produced by chain procedure.

b) Single entry systems fail to correct completely the separations caused by the application of a citation order or significance order; for this, multiple entry systems are necessary.

SIZE

a) A basis for order in array; eg Hand guns, Shoulder guns, Artillery; Mice, Cats, Dogs, Horses (in a classification scheme for Pets).

c) Increasing complexity.

SLIC

a) Selective Listing In Combination: John Sharp's adaptation of Combination indexing, which eliminates redundant entries; eg, if a document is indexed under Cataloguing: Maps: University libraries there is no need to index it also under Cataloguing: Maps, nor under Cataloguing. For the document given as an example under Combination indexing, SLIC would generate only these entries:

1) Cataloguing: Maps: University libraries
2) Cataloguing: University libraries
3) Maps: University libraries
4) University libraries

The number of entries generated is given by 2^{N-1}, where N is the number of elements; with three elements, four entries. In addition, references from synonyms and related classes are necessary, as with combination indexing.

SOUGHT HEADING *see* APPROACH TERM; SOUGHT LABEL

SOUGHT LABEL

a) A heading in an author/title catalogue chosen because it is likely to be looked for by enquirers who want the document, rather than because it represents anybody with intellectual responsibility for the work; eg, the sought label for a Festschrift would be the name of the person in whose honour it has been produced, rather than the editor's name.

SPACE

a) One of Ranganathan's fundamental categories, to which facets representing geographical concepts are assigned.

b) Space is usually fourth in the facet formula represented by PMEST, but it is the primary facet in classes such as History and Law.

SPATIAL PROXIMITY

a) A basis for order in array, resulting in, for example, Stock, Lock, Barrel; or Kent, Surrey, Sussex, Hampshire, Dorset.

SPECIAL CLASSIFICATION SCHEMES

a) Schemes which cover a restricted area of knowledge; eg diamond technology, education, arms and armour, social welfare.

b) Special schemes often draw upon general classification schemes for fringe topics, and for common facets.

SPECIAL (1)

a) Of a species.

SPECIAL (2)

a) Of less extension relative to some other class; eg, the class Middle aged persons is more special than the class Adults.

c) General-special order; Specific.

SPECIALS

a) In CC, specialisms in a discipline to which all the techniques of the discipline may be subordinated; eg, in Medicine, classes such as Paediatrics, Tropical medicine, War medicine, which result in such classes as Anaesthetics for children being collocated with Paediatrics rather than with Anaesthesia.

b) It may be that Specials is an unnecessary concept, the problem being handled perfectly well by ordinary synthesis; should CC7 ever appear it seems likely that Specials will be dropped.

c) Systems.

SPECIES

a) One of the five predicables: a kind of a thing; eg, Timber churches is a species of the genus Churches; Churches is a species

124

of the genus Religious buildings; Flintlock firearms is a species of the genus Firearms; Firearms is a species of the genus Weapons.

b) Species are derived from their genus by the addition of differences.

c) Characteristics of division; Classes; Logical division.

SPECIFIC

a) Co-extensive with a document's subject, or with the subject of an enquiry (used of a descriptor or of an approach term).

c) Special; Specifiers.

SPECIFIC INDEX

a) An alphabetical subject index in which entry words are not qualified, as there is only one notation for each entry word; eg, from SC:

English literature   M521

Poetry   N100

Radio   B637

b) A specific index is efficient only when used for a classification scheme in which each concept appears once only in the schedules—that is, at present, only for a special faceted classification and the obsolete SC. It is obviously not useful as the index to a classified file, because there will be distributed relatives on the shelves and in the classified file (eg, after SC has been applied in a library, not all documents on Poetry will be at N100); and it is similarly unhelpful as the index to an enumerative classification scheme or to a general faceted classification scheme based on main classes. For these purposes a relative index is essential.

SPECIFICATION

a) The statement of a document's subject for indexing purposes, without the display of relationships found in a structured index vocabulary.

b) Specification is sometimes opposed to classification by writers in this field; in fact, specification is an aspect of classification.

SPECIFICITY

a) A quality of an indexing tool or system: the extent to which it can be specific through its index language.

c) Close classification; Precision; Specifiers.

SPECIFIERS

a) Precise statements of a document's subject, not necessarily used as descriptors.

b) In an indexing system whose vocabulary is specific, all descriptors are necessarily specifiers; but not all specifiers are descriptors; for example, a synonym which is not a preferred term is a specifier but not a descriptor. Again, if semantic factors are used, the descriptors are not specifiers and the specifiers are not descriptors: if Fathers is indexed as Males + Parents, Fathers is not a descriptor, and neither of the descriptors is specific.

c) Entry terms.

SPREAD TITLE PAGE

a) An opening (ie two opposite pages of a book) over which the information usually found on the title page alone is spread, without repetition.

b) Distinguish a spread title page from an opening of which one page gives information about the work as part of a series, and the other gives the usual title page information. A spread title page is treated as though the information were on one page.

STANDARD BOOK NUMBER *see* INTERNATIONAL STANDARD BOOK NUMBER

STANDARD CATALOGUING

a) Full cataloguing as opposed to limited cataloguing.

STANDARD CITATION ORDER

a) The generalised citation order Thing-Kinds-Parts-Materials-Properties-Processes-Operations-Agents.

STARS

a) Karen Sparck Jones's name for a group of terms produced by automatic keyword indexing in which each term is allied to the same common term, but not to other members of the star.

c) Cliques; Clumps; Strings.

STARVATION

a) UDC's policy of leaving the notation for a class which has been re-located unused for ten years, so as to allow time for libraries who have used that notation to run down their documents at that number.

c) Integrity of numbers.

STATISTICAL ASSOCIATION *see* ASSOCIATIVE INDEXING SYSTEMS

STEM *see* PARADIGM; TRUNCATION

STEPS OF DIVISION

a) The successive levels of subordinate classes in a hierarchy; eg, those labelled 1), 2) and 3) below:

```
                        Weapons
       ┌───────────────────────┴──────────────────────┐
1) Hand weapons                              Missile weapons
       ┌────────────┴──────────┐           ┌───────────┴──────────┐
2) Armes blanches   Staff weapons       Thrown              Projectile
       │                │               weapons             weapons
    ┌──┴──┐          ┌──┴──┐          ┌────┴────┐         ┌────┴────┐
3) Swords Daggers   Clubs Pikes      Bolas  Boom-       Bows  Firearms
                                             erang
```

c) Characteristics of division; Logical division.

STOP LISTS

a) In mechanised systems, machine-held lists of terms which are not to be used as descriptors—eg, non-significant terms—against which natural language indexing terms can be matched.

STRINGS

a) Karen Sparck Jones's name for groups of terms derived by automatic means in which each term is related to one only of the others.

c) Clumps; Cliques; Stars.

STRIP INDEXES

a) Visible indexes in which entries are made on strips of card allowing for two or three lines of information.

STRUCTURAL NOTATION

a) Notation which displays the generic or syntagmatic structure of the classification scheme, by being hierarchical or expressive or both.

c) Ordinal notation.

STRUCTURED HEADINGS
a) Alphabetical subject headings which abandon ordinary language form when necessary, to achieve the purpose of the index; eg

> Dickens, Charles
> Psychology—Children
> Architecture, Domestic

c) Subheadings (1).

STRUCTURED INDEX VOCABULARIES
a) Those which display relationships between terms, either by juxtaposition—as in systematic catalogues—or by references.

b) Structured vocabularies increase recall, because they remind the searcher of subordinate, superordinate, coordinate and collateral classes which might give more information (eg Mental illness *see also* Schizophrenia), and also increase precision, because they help him to narrow his search.

c) Classification schemes; Controlled index vocabularies; Natural language indexing systems; Search thesaurus; Syndetic structure; Thesauri.

SUBCODES *see* CODING

SUBFACETS
a) A subfacet is a set of classes produced by the application of a single characteristic of division within a facet; eg, the Buildings facet of a classification of architecture might contain subfacets such as buildings by style (giving foci such as Gothic, Baroque); buildings by use (Religious buildings, Educational buildings; Dwellings); buildings by material (Timber buildings, Concrete buildings).

b) Notice that each subfacet exhausts the universe of the facet—for example, all buildings must be built of some material, so all could be accomodated in the buildings by material subfacet.

c) Logical division; Quasi-isolates; Superimposed classes.

SUBHEADINGS (1)
a) Terms added to entry words in alphabetical subject headings either to narrow the extension or to express concepts of form; eg

128

        Papermaking—Dictionaries
        Papermaking—Education
        Papermaking—History
    c) Qualifiers; Roles; Structured headings.

SUBHEADINGS (2)

    a) The names of subordinate bodies added to the name of a corporate author; eg Library Association. *London and Home Counties Branch*

SUBJECT (1)

    a) The information content of a document.
    c) Forms of presentation; Themes.

SUBJECT (2)

    a) A discipline; a subject of study in which one might specialise.
    c) Aspect classification schemes; Basic classes.

SUBJECT (3)

    a) That about which a statement is made; especially in logic.
    c) Predicables; Predicate.

SUBJECT ANALYSIS *see* FACET ANALYSIS; LITERARY WARRANT

SUBJECT CATALOGUES

    a) Those whose file organisation is based on the subject or form of documents, as opposed to author, title, series etc.
    c) Alphabetico-classed catalogues; Alphabetico-direct catalogues; Classified catalogues; Post-coordinate indexing systems; Pre-coordinate indexing systems; Systematic catalogues.

SUBJECT HEADINGS LISTS

    a) Controlled and structured lists of headings for use in alphabetico-direct catalogues; eg, LCSH.
    c) Thesauri.

SUBJECT INDEX *see* ALPHABETICAL SUBJECT INDEXES

SUBJECTIVE INTENSION

a) Those properties of a class which an individual may idiosyncratically associate with it.

SUBORDINATE CLASSES

a) Classes which are wholly included in some other class are said to be subordinate to it; eg, in the hierarchy

```
                    Dwellings
Single dwellings    Multiple dwellings
                    Tenements    Flats
                    Bed sitting rooms
```

the class Bed sitting rooms is subordinate to the class Tenements, the classes Tenements and Flats are subordinate to the class Multiple dwellings; and the classes Single dwellings and Multiple dwellings are subordinate to the class Dwellings.

b) Subordinate classes are of lesser extension but greater intension than their superordinate classes.

c) Collateral classes; Coordinate classes.

SUBSIDIARY AUTHORS

a) Authors other than the principal author in a work of multiple authorship.

c) Secondary authors.

SUBTHEMES

a) The constituents of the theme of a work, used in depth indexing.

b) A work whose theme may be summarised as Cataloguing will probably contain subthemes such as Author cataloguing, Precoordinate subject cataloguing, Post-coordinate subject cataloguing, Descriptive cataloguing, Computerised cataloguing etc.

c) Exhaustive indexing; Exhaustivity.

SUBTITLE

a) A subordinate title whose function is to explain or modify the title; for example, the parts of the transcriptions below which follow the colon:

The quest for Corvo: an experiment in biography
Here I stand: a life of Martin Luther
Information retrieval: notes for students.

b) Distinguish subtitles from alternative titles, and from merely long titles such as *The pilgrim's progress from this world to that which is to come, delivered under the similitude of a dream.*

SUM *see* LOGICAL PRODUCT

SUMMARISATION

a) The statement of the subject of a work as a whole—that is, the statement of its theme—as opposed to depth indexing. Summarisation is the basis of conventional pre-coordinate techniques.

b) Notice that a summarisation may be—should be—specific; for example, the summarisation expressed by the term Cataloguing for John Horner's work of that name is absolutely specific; depth indexing does not increase specificity, only the recall for the sub-themes.

c) Exhaustive indexing; Exhaustivity.

SUPERIMPOSED CLASSES

a) Simple classes defined by more than one characteristic; eg Maladjusted children (people by age and by problem); English gothic cathedrals; French flintlock hunting rifles. A former colleague suggests a test to discover whether one is dealing with a superimposed or composite class: Can one say of it 'x which is/are also y'?; eg, children who are also maladjusted persons; firearms which are French, and also hunting firearms and also flintlock firearms; cathedrals which are also English buildings and also gothic buildings.

b) With faceted classification schemes superimposed classes are expressed by the synthesis of notation for foci from different subfacets within the same facet.

c) Difference; Quasi-isolates; Superimposition (1).

SUPERIMPOSED RANDOM CODING

a) An indirect coding system for item entry cards in which the full set of holes is regarded as a single field, so that any hole is available for coding more than one term.

b) Superimposed random coding allows many more terms to be encoded for a document than do fixed field systems, but causes more false drops. Foskett calculates that the most economical fixed field system, 7–4–2–1, allows six terms for a document entered on a 75 hole card, assuming that up to three digits are allowed for each term (that is, allowing up to 1,000 terms in the index vocabulary). By contrast, superimposed random coding allowing two holes for each term would enable up to 17 terms to be encoded for each document on the same size of card. False drops are reduced by ensuring an even scatter of terms over the available holes, and by leaving about half the holes unused; the result is that the likelihood of two or more concepts sharing the same pair of holes is reduced, but not eliminated.

SUPERIMPOSITION (1)
a) The construction of notation for superimposed classes by synthesis.

SUPERIMPOSITION (2)
a) The use of new cataloguing practices for new accessions, while leaving old entries undisturbed and maintaining a single catalogue.

c) Attrition; No conflict.

SUPERORDINATE CLASSES
a) Classes which wholly include other classes are said to be superordinate to those classes; for example, in the hierarchy

Dwellings
_____
Single dwellings   Multiple dwellings
_____
Tenements   Flats
|
Bed sitting rooms

the class Dwellings is superordinate to all other classes; Multiple dwellings is superordinate to Tenements and Bed sitting rooms, and to Flats; and Tenements is superordinate to Bed sitting rooms.

b) Superordinate classes are of greater extension than their subordinate classes, but of lesser intension.

c) Collateral classes; Coordinate classes.

SUPERORDINATE SEARCH
a) A search broadened from a narrower class to include superordinate classes.

c) Generic search.

SURROGATES

a) Records of documents in catalogues; so called because the records act as substitutes for the documents.

c) Dummy books.

SWITCHING LANGUAGE *see* INTERMEDIATE LEXICON

SYLLABIC NOTATION

a) Notation consisting of letters in pronounceable combinations, as used consistently in LEC1 (LEC2 has partially abandoned it); eg Ruf (= Outward bound schools); Fab (= the teaching profession); Jib (= examinations).

b) Syllabic notation is highly mnemonic, but is also wasteful, inhospitable and, like any notation which attempts to have more qualities than are necessary, probably not worth the extra trouble.

SYNDETIC STRUCTURE

a) Cutter's name for the reference structure which displays relationships in an alphabetical subject catalogue. This seems to be a metaphor—'syndetic' means 'of conjunctions' in the grammatical sense, so perhaps Cutter saw *see* and *see also* references as being analogous to joining words like 'and' and 'but'.

c) Structured index vocabularies.

SYNONYMS

a) Different names for the same concept; eg Underprivileged/Disadvantaged; Underdeveloped countries/Developing countries/Third World; Gramophone/Record player; Staff weapons/Polearms.

b) The failure to control synonyms in natural language indexing systems lowers recall performance; the control of synonyms in a controlled index vocabulary may marginally reduce precision, in that there are very few true synonyms.

c) Homographs.

SYNTAGMATIC RELATIONSHIPS

a) Those relationships between classes which involve interaction, not merely coexistence or the creation of another kind of thing.

b) Syntagmatic relationships produce composite classes; eg, Maladjustment in children; Cataloguing of maps; A comparison between long bows and flat bows.

c) Genus-species relationships; Superimposed classes.

SYNTAX

a) The methods by which relationships between terms in an index vocabulary are displayed, and the rules for the construction of terms which have more than one element.

SYNTHESIS

a) The construction of a notation for a composite or superimposed class by joining the notations for the elements; eg, the class Hypnopaedia in the teaching of history by the Open University would have its notation built up from the following elements (using LEC2):

Nig—History
Sas—Open University
Lak—Sleep teaching

to give the class number SasNigLak.

b) By extension, synthesis can be taken to refer to the construction of alphabetical subject headings in the same way.

c) Faceted classification schemes.

SYSTEMATIC CATALOGUES

a) Pre-coordinate subject catalogues whose entries are in systematic order, so that relationships are displayed by juxtaposition. These usually (but not invariably) have headings in the form of notation from a classification scheme; when this is so, they are known as classified catalogues.

c) Alphabetical subject indexes; Alphabetico-classed catalogues; Alphabetico-direct catalogues; Chain procedure; Relative indexes.

SYSTEMATIC MNEMONICS

a) Mnemonics which result from the use of the same symbols to represent a concept in whatever context it appears; as happens with synthetic notation, and even in enumerative classification schemes if a degree of facet analysis, conscious or unconscious, has taken place; eg, it is not difficult to fill in the blanks in this table, based on DC:

English literature	820
English poetry	821
English drama	822
French literature	840
French poetry	841
French—	842
Italian literature	850
Italian poetry	85–
Italian drama	852

c) Literal mnemonics.

SYSTEMATIC ORDER

a) An order of items which itself displays subject or form relationships; compare the systematic order: Weapons—Projectile weapons—Firearms—Wheellock firearms—Percussion lock firearms; with the non-systematic alphabetical order: Firearms—Percussion lock firearms—Projectile weapons—Weapons—Wheellock firearms.

c) Classification; Collocation; Helpful order.

SYSTEMS

a) In CC, schools of thought, or approaches, in a discipline, to which any focus in the class may be subordinated; eg, in Medicine, systems include Homoeopathy; in Education, Rousseauism, Pestallozzi, Fröbel; in Economics, Socialism, Syndicalism.

b) As with specials, it may seem unnecessary to give a name to this concept: the problem is merely one of synthesis and choice of citation order.

T

TAGS

a) Elements on computer input information which identify the kind of information; eg author tag, series tag, subject tag.

c) Variable fields.

TELEGRAPHIC ABSTRACTS *see* SEMANTIC CODE

TELESCOPING

a) The enumeration of a class which should be expressed by synthesis.

b) Telescoping may be used for two reasons: 1) the composite or superimposed class occurs very commonly, so that it is economical for the indexer to find a notation ready-made; and 2) the class might give rise to dependent classes which could not be included without it; eg the class English secondary schools—a superimposed class—must be listed, before types of secondary schools peculiar to England can be included.

The same principle applies when semantic factors may be used: it may be better to prefer the commonly-occurring term to the semantic factors.

c) Unit concepts.

TERM ENTRY SYSTEMS

a) Post-coordinate indexing systems in which each card represents a concept; numbers which represent documents which deal with that concept are posted on the card.

b) Term entry cards must be kept in order, and a list of document numbers must be kept in addition to the cards, as a link between the index and the documents themselves; on the other hand, in term entry systems the whole file does not need to be searched to satisfy a request, as is the case with item entry systems.

c) Optical coincidence cards; Partitioning; Terminal digit posting; Uniterm cards.

TERM INDEXING *see* NATURAL LANGUAGE INDEXING

TERM ON ITEM *see* ITEM ENTRY SYSTEMS

TERMINAL DIGIT POSTING

a) Posting document numbers on Uniterm cards according to their final digit, so as to ensure a random scatter of numbers across the face of the card and so facilitate the scanning which is necessary with this kind of post-coordinate index; eg see illustration on p. 137.

THEME

a) The summarised statement of a document's subject, which serves as the basis for conventional indexing systems; eg, for a document with chapters on schizophrenia, depression, paranoia etc the theme might be stated as Mental illness.

UNEMPLOYMENT									
0	1	2	3	4	5	6	7	8	9
70	91	22	13	104		56		28	39
	101	82	23			106			53
	111		33						109

c) Depth indexing; Exhaustive indexing; Exhaustivity; Sub-themes.

THESAURI

a) Controlled and structures index languages for use with post-coordinate indexing systems; eg *Thesaurofacet*, TEST.

c) Circular thesaurus; Classification schemes; Intermediate lexicon; Microthesauri; Satellite thesauri; Search thesauri; subject headings lists.

TIME

a) One of Ranganathan's fundamental categories, that to which concepts of time are assigned. It comes last in the facet formula represented by PMEST.

TITLES

a) Names of works.

c) Alternative titles; Subtitles; Title indexing; Uniform titles.

TITLE INDEXING

a) Keyword indexing using terms found in titles.

c) KWIC.

TITLE PAGE
a) The page in a printed book which conventionally gives the formal title, statement of authorship, imprint details and edition; some of this information may appear on the verso.

c) Spread title page.

TRACINGS
a) A record of all the headings generated by a document in a particular catalogue, usually kept on the main entry.

b) Tracings ensure that all records of a document are removed when the document is withdrawn, or amended as necessary.

TRUNCATION
a) A form of confounding by which terms are entered under their stems or roots; so that, for example, a search under Catalog would retrieve documents containing keywords such as Catalogues. Recataloguing, Cataloguing, Precataloguing, Catalogs etc.

c) Paradigm.

U

UNCERTAIN AUTHORSHIP
a) The condition in which the authorship of a work is not certainly known, but has been variously attributed.

c) Anonymous authorship.

UNESTABLISHED SUBJECTS *see* ESTABLISHED SUBJECTS; INDISTINCT SUBJECTS

UNICONCEPTS *see* UNIT CONCEPTS

UNIFORM HEADING
a) In author/title cataloguing, a heading which is always used to represent an entity which has more than one name, or more than one form of name; eg, the preferred pseudonym for an author who writes under more than one; either the family name or the title of a peer; uniform titles.

b) Uniform headings collocate documents, and so produce a bibliographic catalogue.

c) Controlled index vocabularies; Finding list catalogues; Unit of collocation.

UNIFORM TITLE

a) A uniform heading used to collocate entries for all bibliographic units which are manifestations of the same literary unit; eg
[Robinson Crusoe] in:

Defoe, Daniel
[Robinson Crusoe]
A child's Robinson Crusoe . . .

Defoe, Daniel
[Robinson Crusoe]
The life and strange surprising adventures of Robinson Crusoe . . .

Defoe, Daniel
[Robinson Crusoe. French]
Les aventures de Robinson Crusoe . . .

UNINVERTED FILES

a) Computer files in which information is held in item entry form; that is, in document order, with descriptors or specifiers attached.

c) Inverted files.

UNION *see* LOGICAL PRODUCT

UNION CATALOGUE

a) A catalogue which records the holdings of a number of libraries, to act as a locating list. In such catalogues limited cataloguing is usually practised; it is likely that many will become merely lists of ISBNs with locations attached.

UNIQUELY DEFINING CLASS

a) That class which provides the only necessary basis for the definition of another class, and from which it cannot be dissociated; eg, Coal may be of interest to economists, mining engineers, fuel technologists etc, but it is always a geological entity, and Geology is its uniquely defining class.

b) If, as Coates suggests, a grouped alphabetical subject index is used for very large collections, the uniquely defining class will be the fundamental class for entry words. In the proposed CRG general classification scheme, entities which could appear at different integrative levels would be placed at that which corresponds to their uniquely defining class.

UNIT CONCEPT

a) In post-coordinate indexing systems, a descriptor which represents two or more isolates in the index vocabulary; eg, the descriptor Juvenile delinquents, used instead of two entries, one under Young people, the other under Delinquency.

b) Unit concepts represent a degree of pre-coordination in post-coordinate indexes. They may avoid some false drops, and are economic if the concept is a common one, which has to be frequently indexed and frequently searched for; but reduce the recall performance of the index.

c) Semantic factors; Telescoping.

UNIT ENTRIES

a) Copies of the same entry for a document in a catalogue, each of which bears the same information, including the main entry heading; although, of course, each copy will also be given a unique heading under which it will file in the catalogue. BNB cards provide an example.

b) If entries are mechanically produced then there is no reason to have full information on one entry only; it is cheaper and more convenient to run off copies bearing the same information, and better for the catalogue users.

c) Abbreviated entries; Added entries; Alternative entries.

UNIT OF COLLOCATION

a) The set of entries found under one heading in an author/title catalogue.

b) The extent of units of collocation indicates the degree to which the catalogue collocates; for example, the use of uniform headings increases the size of the unit of collocation.

c) Bibliographic catalogues; Uniform title.

UNITERM CARDS
a) Cards for a term entry post-coordinate index, on which document numbers written; eg

c) Optical coincidence cards; Dual dictionaries; Terminal digit posting.

UNNAMED GROUPS
a) An unnamed group which has acted as an author may be assigned a conventional name (as recommended by ALA 1949); or the work may be treated as an anonymous work, and entered under title (AACR 1967).

UNSCHEDULED MNEMONICS *see* SEMINAL MNEMONICS

UNSCHEDULED SUBJECTS
a) Subjects for which no class exists in the classification scheme or other indexing tool.

c) Hospitality; Specificity; Verbal extensions.

UNSOUGHT LINKS
a) In chain procedure: parts of a chain which will not provide entries that enquirers will look under; eg (from UDC):

```
        788    Wind instruments
         .01      Brass
        788.1/.4   SPECIFIC BRASS INSTRUMENTS
        788.2      Trombones
and     750    Painting
         .06      VARIOUS PROBLEMS
          1         Counterfeiting
```

Of course no entries should be made under Specific brass instruments or under Various problems: Painting.

c) False links; Hidden links; Quasi-isolates.

UPWARD REFERENCES
a) *See also* references made from subordinate to superordinate classes, to enable an enquirer to broaden his search in an alphabetical subject catalogue; eg Castles *see also* Military architecture.

b) It is not practical to make references from all possible subordinate classes, so the cataloguer must decide at what level to stop;

alternatively, he could decide to make an upward reference FROM a heading for the book he is cataloguing to the next superordinate class, provided that there is a document at that class.

c) Chain; Downward references; Horizontal references.

USER INTEREST PROFILES *see* PROFILES

V

VDU *see* VISUAL DISPLAY UNIT

VARIABLE FIELDS

a) Fields on computer input media which may vary in length to accommodate information of any extent; for variable fields, tags are necessary.

c) Fixed fields.

VENN DIAGRAMS

a) Diagrammatic representations of logical operations; an example is shown under Logical difference, Logical product and Logical sum.

c) Boolean algebra; Euler circles.

VERBAL EXTENSIONS

a) Word added to a class number which is not specific, to make the subject statement co-extensive with the document's subject; eg, 796.86 Sabre, in which 796.86 = Fencing, and the verbal extension makes it specific for a work on sabre fencing.

b) To preserve systematic order, verbal extensions should modulate; eg, for a work on the Italian school of foil fencing, 796.86 Foil. Italian. Verbal extensions are used in BNB; before 1971, they were introduced by [1].

c) Feature headings; Specificity.

VISIBLE INDEX

a) A physical form of catalogue in which cards are locked into flat trays so that the cards overlap, displaying a strip of card to take the heading; or in which strips of card are inserted in trays, with the same effect; but the first form gives more space for information on the card.

VISUAL DISPLAY UNIT

a) A cathode ray tube on which information from a computer can be displayed, and information from the enquirer input to the computer. This is an on-line device, which allows interaction between the enquirer and the machine during the search, so that search strategy may be modified.

c) Heuristic searches.

VOCABULARY *see* INDEX VOCABULARY

W

WALL-PICTURE PRINCIPLE *see* DEPENDENCE

WEIGHTING

a) A device to increase precision; each descriptor is given a 'score' which indicates the degree of importance of the concept it represents in the document being indexed; in mechanised systems this can be used to rank documents retrieved, according to the weighting assigned to the descriptors which produced them.

c) Links; Roles.

WHOLE NUMBER NOTATION *see* ARITHMETICAL NOTATION

WHOLE TEXT INDEXING

a) Indexing which relies upon the input of all keywords in a document.

WORD FORMS *see* CONFOUNDING; PARADIGM; TRUNCATION

WORD BY WORD

a) A filing method for ordinary language headings, in which the word is regarded as the filing unit; eg

East Ham
Eastbourne

Easte Row
Easter Island
c)   Letter by letter.

WORKING TERMS *see* **DESCRIPTORS**

Z

ZATOCARDS *see* **EDGE NOTCHED CARDS**

WITHDRAWAL